IRVING BERLIN

IRVING BERLIN

From Penniless Immigrant to America's Songwriter

PAUL M. KAPLAN

PELICAN PUBLISHING
New Orleans

For Jiyoung Cha

ISBN 9781455625406
Ebook ISBN 9781455625413

Printed in the United States of America

Published by Pelican Publishing
New Orleans, LA
www.pelicanpub.com

Contents

Preface

Baseball fans sing "God Bless America" at stadiums across the US during the seventh-inning stretch. During times of national tragedies such as September 11, 2001, Americans turn to the familiar song. In December, holiday shoppers hear Bing Crosby's "White Christmas" with its familiar lyrics: "I'm dreaming of a white Christmas, just like the ones I used to know." Entertainers and producers commonly employ the phrase, "There's no business like show business," perhaps unaware of its origins from the 1946 musical, *Annie Get Your Gun*.

Yet few know the story of the man behind these popular tunes. He was Irving Berlin—the personification of a "rags to riches story." His own life played out like a character from one of his songs. His Jewish-Russian family escaped pogroms and immigrated to New York City with scarcely a dollar to their name. Like many immigrant children on the Lower East Side, he dropped out of school at the age of thirteen. Feeling like a burden to his family for his meager income in working odd jobs, he left home for the raucous nearby Bowery Street.

It was in the night cafes where Berlin sang that he discovered his talents. The more he sang the songs customers liked, the more coins they threw at him. The connection between giving audiences what they want with earning more money stayed with Berlin throughout his career. He was, at heart, a commercial songwriter.

His early childhood was typical for an immigrant boy coming to New York City's shores in the late nineteenth century. He lived in the crowded Lower East Side, learned English, and worked odd jobs as a newsie. Yet, in his teens, his life deviated from this path. He discovered his natural talent for songwriting. He never formally studied music. Experimenting on a piano at a bar he worked in, he taught himself to play the instrument—even if he could only play one key. In writing for bar patrons, he realized his knack for creating musical parody, formulating catchy songs, and understanding what the public wanted to hear.

The timing was right for Berlin's entrance in the nascent twentieth century. The music-going public was tiring of Victorian and classical-inspired music. Many were looking for something with more of an edge. They wanted a tune they could dance to. Ragtime music filled this need. Scott Joplin founded the genre known for its syncopated rhythm, but Berlin brought it to the mainstream. After his ragtime mega-hit, "Alexander's Ragtime Band," he became an overnight sensation.

As he matured as a composer, Berlin's music took on an emotional depth. The feelings in his tunes often reflected his personal state. When he endured personal tragedy—as when his first wife died unexpectedly shortly after their honeymoon or his newborn son passed away—he poured his sadness into his songs. Songwriting was his refuge.

Part of his success was adapting to the sweeping changes in the musical tastes of the early-to-mid-twentieth century. He was at one time known as the "ragtime king" and sold millions of copies of sheet music. When radio eclipsed music sales, Berlin changed his business model. When *Ziegfeld Follies* brought the US musical to theater audiences, Berlin was writing tunes for showgirl numbers. Musicals soon became more sophisticated with plot-integrated songs like in *Oklahoma!* and *Show Boat.* Berlin tried to adapt his lyrics, though he was never as comfortable with the plot-integrated music as he was with stand-alone songs. After "talkies" became popular with filmgoers, Berlin wrote music for stars of the day like Fred Astaire, Ginger Rogers, Judy Garland, and Ethel Merman.

In contrast to his contemporaries—George and Ira Gershwin and Cole Porter—Berlin's music tended to be simpler in both composition and lyric. His songs were relatable to the average American. Berlin always said his ambition was to "reach the heart of the average American." His aim was also to sell music.

But the music stopped by the mid-1950s with the advent of rock and roll. Elvis Presley and hits like Bill Haley and His Comets' "Rock Around the Clock" reinvented music. This time, Berlin was out of step. But over a half-century later, his songs live on in an ever-changing musical landscape.

Enjoy the story.

Acknowledgments

Thanks to Rich Boursy, archivist at the Irving S. Gilmore Music Library at Yale University, for curating letters and telegrams written by Berlin. Thanks also to Christina Kasman, formerly of the Yale Club of New York City's library as well as the staff of the Library of Congress, Division of Prints and Photographs. I also acknowledge the contributions of authors of previous biographies and documentaries on Berlin. Thanks also to Eileen Kaplan for her editing and content suggestions and Karen Seiger, editor of 111 Places travel guides, for her support.

A shout-out to the team at Pelican Publishing and Arcadia/History Press, including Pelican editor in chief Nina Kooij and assistant editor Matt Wilson, Pelican sales director John Scheyd, and publicist Maddison Potter.

I also thank key venues for book talks including the Harvard Club, Yale Club, Union League of New York, Greenwich Village Society for Historic Preservation, Elm City Club, General Society of Mechanics & Tradesmen, Jewish Museum of Florida, Lower East Side Conservancy, Museum at Eldridge Street, and many more. Also thanks to Writer's Voice for this fine radio show's support of my other book projects.

Thanks also to all my friends, colleagues, and family for their support.

Chapter 1

Immigrating to America

The cold winter air swept through the Russian plains. Most days were freezing in the quiet, small town of Mogilev, situated in Russia's Pale of Settlement. Residents of the area between the Baltic and the Black Sea were used to frigid temperatures.

But on this night something was different. A five-year-old Israel Baline (who would later become Irving Berlin) and his family had gone to bed. In the distance, his father Moses heard wild men on horses. The trotting of horses and shots of rifles drew nearer. Moses feared the worst. He remembered the assassination of the emperor of Russia, Alexander II, twelve years earlier in 1881. That czar had been tolerant of many groups and instituted reforms. But after he was assassinated, Alexander III took a hardline view and issued policies of political repression.

Moses glanced outside his small hut and saw horsemen sweeping through his town, attacking anyone they saw, and scattering livestock from farms. Eerily, he saw flames coming from neighbors' houses. The horsemen were setting homes on fire.

Moses and his wife raced to gather their six children. As they ran outside, the howls and shouts of their neighbors grew louder. There was no place to hide. Lena Baline, Israel's mother, put down a blanket and tried wrapping it around her children. The family watched their neighborhood burn to the ground. Moses and his wife knew what would happen next. The men stopped at the home of the Balines. The family looked on helplessly as their shack went up in flames. "Huddled in a blanket and clinging to his mother, little Israel Baline stared wide-eyed at the flames. He heard laughter, shouting, and screams."[1] By morning, the house was nothing but ashes.

It was 1893. Pogroms like these were common against Jews and other ethnic minorities. Families thought they were relatively safe in towns like Mogilev. They worshipped and conducted their business in relative peace. Or so they thought.

The Balines were suddenly homeless. Moses was a cantor who sang prayers during religious services at Jewish synagogues. He loved music, but he earned little money from it. So he could not afford to rebuild his house. Moses looked around his neighborhood. It was a heap of ashes. He knew he had to leave at once. Russia, he realized, was no longer safe. But with virtually no money and few skills, his prospects were dim.

Then he remembered his cousin who lived in New York City. He had heard of other Russians immigrating to the United States. From what he heard, the US, or Amerike in Yiddish, was full of opportunity. He heard others call it the "Golden Land." But he knew that this Golden Land of opportunities probably did not apply to cantors.

America was in everybody's mouth, recalled a young Russian. She wrote,

> People who had relatives in the famous land went around reading their letters for the enlightenment of less fortunate folks . . . Children played at emigrating; old folks shook their sage heads over the evening fire, and prophesized no good for those who braved the terrors of the sea . . . All talked about it, but scarcely anyone knew one true fact about this magic land.[2]

Nevertheless, Moses was determined to bring his family to America. So he saved his pennies and eventually accumulated enough money to purchase tickets for his family on a steamship, the SS *Rhynland.* The journey to the US would cost the family around $270 (or about $7,000 in current dollars). So the Balines said one final goodbye to the area they had lived in and known almost their whole lives. The Pale of Settlement in Russia was their whole world. But Moses had his love for music. He sang to bring comfort to his family as they trekked westward to Antwerp, Belgium, where they boarded a vast steam-powered ship built to carry immigrants across the Atlantic Ocean.

The frightened Balines spent more than eleven long days at sea. They traveled in steerage, the least expensive and roughest part of the ship, with crowds everywhere and endless days on the open sea.

One writer has described the wretched journey faced by immigrants during this period:

> The immigrants faced two weeks to a month of rough seas, crammed together, giving birth, getting sick, dying in the same dank quarters. Often these quarters were filthy. Lice and vermin were common, and

> the food, if it didn't run out, was hardly gourmet . . . The crossing was a miserable ordeal of nausea, fear of what was to come, and seemingly endless days on the open sea.[3]

One night when Israel Baline (called Izzy) was sleeping, another passenger accidentally dropped a knife from an upper bunk and gashed the child's forehead. Adding to the misery, many passengers on the ship were very sick. After more grueling days, the ship finally reached American shores, where the Statue of Liberty beckoned. The boat pulled into the busy harbor. From the decks the passengers saw tall buildings. It was a new sight for many. Passengers felt a strange combination of emotions: thrills, fear, and uncertainty. For Moses, it was a new start. But there was no guarantee his family would be admitted to the new land.

When the Balines reached New York, they joined German, Italian, Irish, and other Russians to be processed in extensive lines at Ellis Island, an immigration processing center. The lines were slow and long. Immigration officers barked directions to the weary Balines in a language that was strange to them: English.

The Balines were held in a pen and inspected for diseases. Everything they owned was stuffed into eight pieces of luggage. Anyone with infectious maladies like tuberculosis, cholera, or typhus was sent back. Exhausted from their journey and almost penniless, if the Balines were rejected entry they had no backup plan. Because immigration officials sent some families back home and divided others, some termed the place Heartbreak Island or Island of Tears.

Moses waited for what seemed like an eternity for each of his six children to pass inspection. As far as Moses knew, his whole family was healthy. But he realized that any one of them could have easily picked up a disease on the treacherous journey to New York.

After inspecting each member, the immigration officials waved them through. The relieved family steered through the crowds and made their way onto to a ferry bound for the island of Manhattan. Their journey was over.

The Balines met their cousin at the ferry dock. As was common practice for family members of newly arrived immigrants, the cousin had found them housing. It was a basement apartment on Monroe Street on the Lower East Side.

The weary family stumbled onto the bustling streets of New

York City to make their way to their new apartment. New York was confusing for these country people. The Lower East Side streets were crowded with ragged immigrants selling from their pushcarts and speaking in foreign languages. The roaring trains, the screeching streetcars, the constant clanking of horses and wagons, and the elevated trains running past the tenements were a striking contrast to the quiet countryside they had fled. Most in their town back home were Russian-Jewish. But here people were from all over the world. The Balines spoke only Yiddish, and their clothes seemed out of place.

Manhattan was a stewpot of diversity. It was said that "you could scream here and no one cared. Because everyone was screaming."[4]

After a short while, the Balines moved around the corner to an equally dark and drab tenement at 330 Cherry Street above Radlow's Fancy Grocery. Their tiny new apartment had no hot water, windows, or electricity. The neighborhood was crowded. By 1900, the Lower East Side had become one of the most populated two-square miles on the face of the Earth with more than a quarter of a million people living per square mile in five out of the eight local wards. To give an idea of how dense that is, today there is an average of seventy

New York's Lower East Side in 1895, where Irving Berlin's family initially settled from Russia. (Courtesy of Library of Congress, Prints and Photographs Division)

thousand residents per square mile in Manhattan. Streets were full of vendors selling goods from their carts lining the neighborhood.

The family's third-floor apartment "consisted of four cramped rooms, small boxes in which eight people lived, worked, and slept. One of the rooms would be the kitchen, equipped with a wood-burning stove; water was drawn from a faucet in the hall. Outhouses were typically in the courtyard at the rear of the tenement; overhead, the courtyard would be webbed by clotheslines, and the ground all around cluttered with carts, pails, and children at play."[5] The children shared beds as was common practice at the time. Still, it was a step up from their basement apartment on Monroe Street. The rent was $9 per month (about $250 in present dollars). As many did, they took in a boarder to help pay for the costly rent.

Lena Baline looked out her window at her bustling new neighborhood. It was a sight completely foreign to one who had spent her life in a small Russian village. She ventured downstairs to buy some groceries

Children are sewing in a tenement doubling as a small sweatshop for clothing manufacturing. The Baline siblings had comparable jobs in the Lower East Side. (Library of Congress, Division of Prints and Photographs)

to cook a meal. She walked a few blocks in the neighborhood. She saw streams of immigrant families from all over Europe.

Narrow brick tenements—their windows open for air—formed a high wall along the streets. There were "no parks, no trees, and no playgrounds. Children fought and played in a stream of traffic. Vendors offered their fruit and vegetables from carts lining the sidewalks. The smell of home cooking and rotting garbage filled the alleys, streets, and apartment halls."[6] On many corners, newsboys hawked the daily paper shouting headlines at passersby. Saloons were on most blocks—to the chagrin of some—as drinking beer was safer than consuming water.

The Cherry Street area located by the East River was also popular with sailors looking for their next drink, a brawl, or prostitution. Nevertheless, the area was popular with indigent, young, immigrant families.

Children toil in a cigar making factory in the Lower East Side in 1889 when labor and child exploitation were common. (Courtesy Visiting Nurse Service of New York Records Archives & Special Collections, Health Sciences Library, Columbia University)

Many immigrants in the area took jobs as peddlers, tailors, garment makers, cigar rollers, or "runners" of garment pieces to different factories. There was a strong demand for cheap labor. But not for cantors. Consequently, Moses Baline could not find work in his new country. Also, the Balines' timing for coming to America was poor. In 1893, the nation was stricken by a severe financial panic followed by an economic depression. Jobs, which were always hard to find, became even scarcer.

He eventually found employment as a kosher meat inspector and later as a housepainter. But he barely got to use what he knew best: singing music.

The children were put to work as well. Izzy's sisters wrapped cigars in a factory, and his brother toiled in a sweatshop making shirts. Children working long hours was common in the neighborhood. Many children had to drop out of school to earn money for their families to supplement their parents' meager earnings. To supplement each family member's income, the Balines reluctantly sold some of their few possessions.

One bright spot for Moses was that he got to sing in a synagogue choir. Izzy would sometimes visit. It was there that Izzy learned to love music.

Chapter 2

Finding Work on the Bowery

Izzy attended school, but he was not much of a student. He was bored. He didn't care much for learning about things that were abstract. *He wanted to do, not study.* Do what, he wasn't sure. But he knew that solving problem sets, reading, and writing were not very interesting. His family also expected him to earn money. So after school he joined the ranks of the newsies who sold newspapers on the streets to passersby.

Izzy was small and feeble. But he learned English fairly fluently. He stood for hours on street corners calling out the day's headlines hoping to entice someone to buy the papers. Selling newspapers was a very rough business. The costs to the newsies for purchasing the papers or the "wholesale cost" was high. Therefore, their profit from selling to customers was low. Worse yet, newsies were often stuck with the papers they could not sell. They had to absorb the cost as the newspaper publishers refused to refund them. As a result, newsies tended to live in squalid conditions. Some undermined each other by cutting retail prices. There were also incidents of newsies pickpocketing their unsuspecting customers.

Izzy found a way to differentiate himself among the scores of other newsies—through singing. Like his father, he had a pleasant voice. He didn't think of it as a way to drum up business; singing helped combat boredom. Passersby started to notice, so Izzy sang more and learned new songs. Since many of the customers were of German, Italian, or Irish descent, he learned songs popular in those communities. Sometimes, smiling onlookers would toss a coin or two at him. Izzy understood if he could sing well and please his audiences, he could make money. It seemed easier and more fun than toiling in sweatshops like his siblings.

This realization was pivotal for the young Izzy. He had always enjoyed music when he heard his father sing at the synagogue as a

Photograph depicting newsies taking a break from hawking newspapers around 1915. Photographer Lewis Hine served on staff for the National Child Labor Committee. (Courtesy Whitney Museum of American Art in New York City)

cantor. Music was his comfort. But Izzy had never thought of it as an occupation.

In the 1890s, many families in impoverished neighborhoods expected their children to work—schooling was secondary. Though it was the law for children eight to sixteen to attend school, it was rarely enforced. Families had more practical needs. In some cases, they would encourage their children to lie about their age or weight in order to secure various jobs. Children were expected to add their meager earnings to the family pool.

Izzy followed this tradition. Every day, he dutifully delivered the few pennies he earned to his family. But it did not help much. When Izzy was nine, tragedy struck. His twenty-year-old sister Sifre died. The cause was likely tuberculosis, also known as the tailor's plague. Tuberculosis is air-borne and passed through tiny droplets of an affected person's coughing, sneezing, talking, singing, or the like. Therefore, given the indoors and close person-to-person workplace setting of tailors in the Lower East Side, this disease was commonly spread. Indeed, cholera, typhus, and small pox took a heavy toll.

Many immigrants were unaware of standard hygiene practices. They sometimes consumed contaminated food or milk, though when pasteurizing milk became standard practice drinking it became safer. Many residents could not afford medical treatment. Almost none had health insurance.

This period was called the Progressive Era (1890-1920) as it ushered in sweeping new reforms. Many of these would help the Balines and families like them. Eventually, the Tenement House Act of 1901 was passed that forced major changes in tenements. Landlords had to provide windows facing outdoors, indoor bathrooms, adequate ventilation, and fire safeguards for safe exits.

To combat many of the illnesses and inadequate housing, some reformers set up settlement houses. They were nurses or educators who lived within the neighborhoods they served. Their efforts were the start of social work and public health. One such settlement was located just a few blocks from the Balines on Henry Street. It was started by an enterprising nurse named Lillian Wald. She trained as a nurse but was disillusioned by what she saw as a stodgy, institutional system. She felt healthcare practitioners did not care for patients' emotional needs. They solved only the symptoms not the causes. So with funding from philanthropists, she set up an apartment near the Balines with her fellow nursing student Mary Brewster. They checked in on neighbors who were reported ill. They also tried to offer financial assistance and coaching. Many patients worked in sweatshops making garments or rolling cigars like the Baline children.

Later, they expanded into the Henry Street Settlement. They partnered with Metropolitan Life Insurance to provide affordable insurance to residents. Importantly, they made sure the communications were in local languages like Yiddish, German, Polish, Greek, or Italian and conveyed images that residents would relate to. The effort was considered a successful public-private venture.

The Settlement also taught classes for youth and adults in English language and in the arts. Classes were racially integrated which was somewhat unusual at the time. It's unclear if the Henry Street Settlement assisted the Balines, but it's quite possible.

Today, the Henry Street Settlement still serves local residents. It split off into the Visiting Nurse Service which visits patients in their homes around the US.

Besides strained finances, the Balines had a new problem. Moses was suffering from bronchitis from the dust he breathed while painting. He had an unshakable cough and shortness of breath. Leg pains made walking and going up stairs difficult. His wife asked local charities for help. Many had been set up for this purpose. He had left Russia for safer and fruitful opportunities. Ironically, in this new land his health was deteriorating. By 1901, his largely untreated condition worsened. In July, he died.

His family was devastated—financially and emotionally. Moses was their stabilizing force. His widow, Lena, aged fifty-three, had no skills and spoke very little English. She was left alone to care for her large family. Though she had been living in New York for about eight years, she had never adjusted to the new land. She missed her homeland. But she knew she'd never get to see it again.

Izzy was now thirteen. His brother Ben toiled in a local shirt factory. His other siblings worked in garment and cigar factories. He was the only child without a job. He felt like a financial burden to his family. As was common then, he saw his living at home as taking up valuable space and resources. So he quit school to work additional hours in order to contribute more money to his impoverished family. In addition to selling newspapers, he now delivered telegrams and sewed collars in a sweatshop. As a newsie, he worked the beat beneath the Brooklyn Bridge peddling the *New York Evening Journal.* He'd shout, "Paper, boss, paper, ma'am." He sold the paper for about one cent but spent a half-cent to buy the paper wholesale. Newsies had only recently earned the ability to return unsold papers. After a long battle in 1899, publishers had reluctantly agreed to take back unsold copies.

The value of those hard-earned pennies is illustrated by an event in young Izzy's life. One day while sitting on a pier he was distracted by a boat and a crane knocked him into the river. He flailed in the cold, dirty waters until he was rescued by an Irishman and rushed to the hospital. "I was scared. More scared than at any time," he later recalled. The nurses discovered clutched in his hand the four pennies he earned from selling papers earlier that evening. That night, he dutifully deposited those coins to his mother.

Even with taking on additional jobs, he was earning less than his siblings who still were toiling in sweatshops and cigar rolling factories. Now age fourteen, Izzy had to face a key decision. Should he stay at home?

His mother and siblings took subsistence jobs typical of immigrants in the Lower East Side at the time. Now a widow, his mother became a midwife. She never learned English very well and, after many years of living in the US, still felt like an outsider.

Izzy felt like a burden to his family. He reasoned that his family would be better off without him. So he decided to leave home. Just as his father left Mogilev a decade earlier with his family for a better life, so set forth Izzy.

But this time Izzy was alone and virtually penniless. He had to think about where to lay his head at night. So he joined the thousands of homeless boys around the rough-and-tumble Bowery Street. As one biographer explained, "Not far from his house on Cherry Street, the Bowery was a long and wide avenue with laundries, boardinghouses, pawnshops, and bars."[1] Here, Izzy tried to find a new life. He slept in cheap rooming houses called flophouses. He said about one place, "You got a cubbyhole to sleep in, and you were always scared that somebody would reach over and steal your pants."[2]

He had to find a way to earn money. Without money, he wouldn't be able to stay in the flophouse. He had no education and no real skills except one: singing. He had realized before that when he sang tunes, customers sometimes tossed coins at him. Now he saw that the more he sang, more customers bought his newspapers. One night while selling newspapers, a passerby said to him, "Go down to the Bowery and get some change. They are looking for good singers there. Get busy and butt in."

Izzy discovered that the Bowery neighborhood was the entertainment district for the working classes, especially for newly arrived immigrants. It was a "paradise of beer saloons, bar-rooms, concert and dance halls, cheap theaters, and low-class shows."[3] Audiences did not have to know English well to enjoy the shows.

The Bowery was not far from his home on Cherry Street. But it seemed a world away. His old neighborhood was teeming with immigrants speaking multiple different languages. Pushcarts were everywhere. It was impoverished and unhygienic. But there was a simple sense of security Izzy felt there. His family lived there and he was used to its hectic space.

But on the Bowery it seemed different. To a fourteen year old—and even to many adults—it was more intimidating. His old neighborhood had boisterous gangs, but the Bowery seemed to have more. The people on the street looked rougher. Pawnshops and bars dotted the wide avenues. Saloons seemed like they were everywhere. Each had a small swinging door that customers, mostly men, entered through. Inside, most had simple tables and chairs on a wooden floor. A bartender stood behind a long, narrow bar. Customers stood around it drinking from bottles, swapping stories and jokes, laughing, and sometimes shouting or even fighting. Some crowds got rowdy particularly as the night grew older.

The rough nature inspired a song from the producer and playwright Charles Hoyt:

> The Bow'ry, the Bow'ry!
> They say such things and they do strange things on the Bow'ry
> The Bow'ry!
> I'll never go there anymore!

Observing this new neighborhood, Izzy noticed something in many of the bars though that gave him comfort. In the back was often an upright piano on a small open space for patrons to listen or dance. Hearing music reminded him of his father. Better yet, it was something that Izzy could relate to and maybe perform for money.

But he still needed to find a place to sleep. Searching up and down the Bowery, Izzy finally found a suitable boardinghouse. For a few cents per night, he got to sleep in a narrow bed with a blanket that was usually dirty. The boardinghouse was crowded and noisy. Izzy would drift off to sleep and hope that none of the residents stole his few possessions.

One evening, as Izzy was selling papers to patrons at saloons, he noticed young children earning money by singing show tunes. "Buskers," as they were called, would be paid by Broadway producers to sing in public places to gain interest in attending shows. Promoters of musicals or variety shows hoped that by hiring these boys to sing tunes to patrons, they would catch on. Buskers were told: "Belt out the verses until the customers know them by heart." There was no radio yet and limited phonographs so the only way a customer could hear a tune was either by playing it at home (and buying the sheet music) or attending the show or concert in which it was played.

Seeing his chance, Izzy jumped at the opportunity to become a busker as well. He remembered the advice that passersby had given him: to try his luck at singing. He did some quick calculations. If he could earn fifteen cents, he could rent a bed in a flophouse with a locker for his clothes. But if he received only five cents, he would have to sleep on the flophouse floor. His clothes would likely be stolen by morning.

Izzy joined these ranks. He hoped that after singing a few tunes, customers would toss coins at him. It seemed like an easier job than selling newspapers or working in a sweatshop.

So Izzy sang for customers at various bars. He borrowed renditions from famous performers at the time like George Cohan who, unbeknownst to him, would one day become his mentor. He sang Cohan's "Give My Regards to Broadway." Today, a statue of Cohan stands in the center of Times Square.

Customers usually liked Izzy's singing. They would toss coins at him just like when he was selling newspapers. When he sang songs they liked he earned more. It was here that Izzy had an important realization: singing popular music made him more money. If he could figure out what patrons wanted, he could earn more. That observation would stay with him for his musical career.

As Izzy visited different bars, the coins kept coming. He started earning enough to pay for his bed and food. Music, he decided, would be his future—never mind that he could neither read nor write music.

The Bowery neighborhood he worked in was the rough part of town, but Izzy started learning its ways. He sang in most of the saloons on the Bowery and knew most of the waiters, bartenders, and customers. He had a faculty for remembering tunes and lyrics and belted out a variety of songs. Some were comic satires, others ballads, and still others had a patriotic flair. Sometimes customers would request a song and he could come up with new lyrics spontaneously.

He realized that dreaming up new tunes could earn him even more. Besides, for the budding songwriter, dreaming up new lyrics was more fun than memorizing someone else's. He worked in several saloons where he learned which songs entertained patrons and earned him more money. In these halls, he taught himself the piano. Since he had no formal instruction, he never learned to play the piano that thoroughly though. He was only ever able to play the black keys.

Although music was not something he formally studied, Izzy had something that can't be taught. He had an intuitive feel for rhythm and lyrics. He tried his hand at a few unmemorable songs. A promoter gave him advice he always remembered: "Give the public what it wants."

Chapter 3

Show Business Bound

Izzy wanted to leave the saloon scene and try his hand at show business. He caught a small break in singing in the chorus of a traveling musical called *The Show Girl.* It was a chance for Izzy to branch out of singing prescribed tunes for often inebriated customers in saloons. Now, he was going to be in a real musical.

But the opportunity was short-lived. Ticket sales were disappointing. Consequently, the show producers cut some of the chorus—including Izzy's part.

So Izzy found himself out of work again. He didn't want to go back to selling newspapers and busking out songs. He wanted steady work in show business. He needed the stability. Izzy had long heard of Harry Von Tilzer, one of the better-known song producers. He worked in New York City's Tin Pan Alley.

At this time, the music scene was dominated by a Manhattan block of music publishers known for the constant clatter from the pianos and percussions resembling banging on tin pans in an alleyway. It was nicknamed Tin Pan Alley. Much of the sheet music enjoyed around the world was produced here.

In the late nineteenth century, middle class families began buying pianos for their parlors. To make use of their pianos, they needed to purchase sheet music to play their favorite songs and for family sing-alongs. Sold in drug stores throughout the country, sheet music became big business. A song could sell as many as 600,000 copies at nine cents per copy. To promote a song, Tin Pan Alley publishers hired "pluggers" to play and sing their new songs at saloons and concert halls.

Making his way through the unfamiliar neighborhood of Tin Pan Alley, an uneasy Izzy entered the office of music publisher Harry Von Tilzer on West 28th Street. He had never been to a music publisher's office before. In fact, he had hardly been to offices at all. As he

Tin Pan Alley dominated the national songwriting business. At its prime before radio, it sought to maximize sales of the sheet music it produced and artfully illustrated. (Courtesy of Wikimedia)

approached the office, he started to wonder, "Who am I but a teenage busker working at saloons?" He worried whether his clothes were up to par.

After explaining to the receptionist what he was there for, he waited for what seemed an eternity. Izzy started doubting himself again. But he remembered how his customers liked his singing and his impromptu songwriting. So why couldn't he write songs? He remembered the advice a promoter had given him. "Give the public what it wants."

Finally, Izzy was shown to Von Tilzer's office. After shaking hands, Von Tilzer cut to the chase. He was a busy man and had no time for chit chat. He had been in the business for a long time. He still felt a little cheated from writing the hit song in 1898, "My Old New Hampshire Home," about a victory in the Spanish-American War. It sold a staggering two million copies. But Von Tilzer earned a measly five dollars. He soon learned that he needed to become a publisher.

He asked the young man to sing. So a nervous Izzy sang a tune from

George Cohan, one of his favorite composers. The song was "Give My Regards to Broadway," which he had performed as a singing waiter.

After a few verses, Von Tilzer had heard enough. He raised his hand for Izzy to stop. He hired Izzy to be a "plugger" of his songs at a local music hall for five dollars per week.

The job seemed easy. Izzy was to watch a play from the balcony. Towards the end of the show, he would stand up, clap, and repeat the song. The key was to sing the song passionately so audiences would remember it—and then buy the sheet music for it. Producers calculated that if patrons loved at least one song in the show they were more likely to recommend the show. That was a cheaper way to bring in new patrons than advertising.

The show Izzy was to plug was a vaudeville act at the well-known Tony Pastor Music Hall. Popular at the time, vaudeville was a variety act show, often featuring acrobats, musicians, jugglers, dancers, singers, or family acts. It was not a show with a straight narrative; rather, vaudeville had a series of acts meant to entertain audiences. For many, it was much needed family entertainment rather than the more risqué burlesque theater or minstrel shows that mocked Blacks relentlessly.

Izzy left Von Tilzer's office empowered. He was going to be in a show—even if just as a plugger. He eagerly awaited the first night's performance to arrive. The show, "The Three Keatons," was a family act as was common among vaudeville shows. The performers did some comedy, juggling, and singing. Throughout the act, Izzy waited nervously in the audience for his song to come up. He kept wondering if audiences would mind if he stood up and started singing the song. Maybe they would find him distracting? Boo him? He had little experience in theaters like these.

Then, the big song came. Uncertain, Izzy stood up in the theater as he had been instructed. He belted out the tune he had practiced. The patrons in the theater were unperturbed by Izzy's performance. In fact, many joined in the singing. Audiences liked his performance. More importantly, they were humming his song as they left the theater. That was always a good sign that they would later purchase the sheet music.

After the show closed, Izzy was out of work again. Yet he had a newfound confidence. He knew he could sing and possibly make up lyrics. Plus, he had taught himself the piano—or at least the black keys.

He found new work at the Pelham Café in Chinatown as a singing waiter for seven dollars per week. The hours were grueling, starting six

Joseph Hart, an American vaudevillian entertainer, manager, producer, and songwriter in New York. (Courtesy of Library of Congress, Division of Prints and Photographs)

Vaudeville offered a variety of entertainment in one show. Trapeze artists, costumed actors, clowns, and dancers were some examples. Types of acts included "popular and classical musicians, singers, dancers, comedians, trained animals, magicians, ventriloquists, strongmen, female and male impersonators, acrobats, illustrated songs, jugglers, one-act plays or scenes from plays, athletes, lecturing celebrities, minstrels, and movies."[1]

Vaudeville developed from a variety of sources including the concert saloon, minstrel shows, dime museums to see natural curiosities, freak shows, and the American burlesque, which usually attracted a more rowdy crowd. For many decades, vaudeville was one of the most popular entertainment forms in the US.

Box office for "Grand" vaudeville show in New York around 1910. (Courtesy Library of Congress, Division of Prints and Photographs)

New York's Pell Street near the Bowery in Chinatown in 1905 where Irving Berlin began his music career. (Courtesy of Library of Congress, Prints and Photographs Division)

or seven at night until eight the following morning. He served patrons their food, drinks, and a healthy dose of music. Working the night shifts, Izzy became an insomniac—a habit he would have the rest of his life. Chinatown had a mystique about it. It had some restaurants and cafés that patrons would frequent after theaters had closed for the night. They found Chinatown's foods and aesthetic different from what they were used to. Parts of it were dangerous with street gangs. Still, it felt classier than Bowery Street. As far as Izzy was concerned, the Pelham was a step up from the saloons he had been playing in.

Customers liked Izzy's singing and especially the lyrics he made up in the spur of the moment. They found many to be funny. More coins were being tossed Izzy's way. They bought more drinks. The owner, Mike Salter, was pleased.

It was also here that Izzy taught himself to compose new songs on the piano. His self-taught music skills paid off as Salter wanted some original songs for his café. After all, patrons could hear popular songs in many places. Noting Izzy's facility for creating songs, he asked Izzy to make up a song with the café's piano player, Nick Nicholson.

New York's Chinatown in 1903. Due to the Chinese Exclusion Act, there were few immigrants coming from China at the time. (Courtesy of Library of Congress, Prints and Photographs Division)

Salter's Café and the Pelham Saloon in Chinatown, New York City in 1905; Berlin worked at a café nearby that looked very similar. (Courtesy of Library of Congress, Prints and Photographs Division, New York World-Telegram & Sun Collection)

So Izzy banged out his first song with Nick helping with the melody. The song was "Marie from Sunny Italy." Local Italian immigrants identified with it.

The song went:

Oh, Marie, 'neath the window I'm waiting
Oh, Marie, please don't be so aggravating
Can't you see my heart just yearns for you, dear
With fond affection
And love that's true, dear
Meet me while the summer moon is beaming
For you and me, the little stars are beaming
Please come out tonight, my queen
Can't you hear my mandolin?

My sweet Marie from sunny Italy
Oh how I do love you

Say that you'll love me, love me, too
Forever more I will be true
Just say the word and I will marry you
And then you'll surely be
My sweet Marie from sunny Italy

Oh, Marie, I've been waiting so patiently
Oh, Marie, please come out and I shall happy be
Raise your window, love, and say you're coming
The little birds, dear
Are sweetly humming
Don't say, "No," my sweet Italian beauty
There's not another maiden e'er could suit me
Come out, love, don't be afraid
Listen to my serenade

The song's lyrics were over-the-top and sentimental. But they carried the Italian dialect that Italian listeners enjoyed. It would serve as an answer to Salter's competitor dance halls that were making their own Italian dialect songs.

But Izzy wanted more than to give his employer a competitive advantage. He wanted to write down the song and sell it. He envisioned that the song would be produced in sheet music and sold throughout the region with his name on it. But there was one problem: Izzy could not read or write music. So with Nick's help, the two brought the song to the music publisher Joseph Stern. Mr. Stern liked the song but was unsure how it would sell. He decided to give it a shot. Rather than paying the songwriters royalties, he offered them a one-time fee of seventy-five cents. It was not a great deal in that if the song sold well, Nick and Izzy would not get to share in those profits. Still, it would be Izzy's first published piece of music. Izzy and Nick agreed to share the seventy-five cents.

Stern wanted the young songwriter to have a catchier name than Israel Baline (Izzy's given name). After all, this was showbiz. So Izzy came up with a more popular—and less ethnic—name: Irving Berlin. Izzy, now going by Irving Berlin, spread a rumor, according to some sources. The rumor was that a printing error created his "pen name."

The song's sheet sales were lackluster. Still, it was his first published song. Plus, now he had a stage name. In 1911, he legally changed his name to Irving Berlin.

Through an unfortunate set of circumstances, the newly named Irving Berlin was fired from his job at Pelham Café. The owner, Mike Salter, asked him to work an extra-long night shift. He was to sweep up the back room, provide beer for the early morning commuters on their way to work (or back home), and to guard the cash register. Unaccustomed to working a twelve-hour shift, Berlin fell asleep on the job. Salter arrived back at the café in the early morning to find twenty-five dollars missing. He blamed Berlin—without real evidence—and fired him on the spot, ordering him not to return.

Chapter 4

Berlin's First Hit

So Berlin left tumultuous Chinatown for a singing waiter job in Union Square. He composed a few more published songs, mostly parodies. With its prime location, many vaudeville and music stars would walk over to the restaurant after their performance. They liked to hear singing waiters. Irving Berlin entertained them week after week. One of his most famous parodies was of "Are You Coming Out Tonight" by Max Winslow.

Soon after, Winslow heard that a singing waiter was parodying one of his songs. Unsure what to do, Winslow ventured to Jim Kelly's restaurant. He was impressed by Berlin's delivery. It was funny, upbeat, and relatable. Customers were engaged. Many were joining in or banging on their tables in time to the music.

Winslow introduced himself to Berlin, and the two quickly became good friends. Soon after, they ended up renting an apartment together. They worked on songs together. This arrangement opened up a new world for Berlin. No longer was he the outsider looking in at the music industry trying to get scraps. Now, with Winslow, he was meeting musicians, singers, and theater producers. He was starting to make a name for himself.

Winslow recommended to Von Tilzer that his company hire the young Berlin as a staff lyricist for fifteen dollars per week. Von Tilzer was not interested. He declined to offer Berlin employment.

Undeterred, Winslow introduced him to his employer, the music publisher Waterson & Snyder. He also introduced Berlin to Edgar Leslie, a music composer. Leslie and Berlin started composing. Their first song was titled "Wait, Wait, Wait." The two wanted to sell the tune. They pitched it to none other than Henry Von Tilzer. He bought the song and Berlin received $200 plus his part of the royalties.

Music publishers were in a very competitive business. They could never tell which songs would become a hit. Profit margins were tight.

However, there was money to be made. Von Tilzer sold over five million music sheets in his first year as a publisher. Part of his success was in having famous singers perform the music and for pluggers to sing excerpts to draw in potential customers. Like much of show business back then and today, most productions did not do well. Songwriters typically wrote many songs that lost money.

Some musicians and songwriters saw making music as their vocation. They wanted to bring beauty and expression through songs. Others were hoping to bring social change through music. For Tin Pan Alley and some of its musicians, though, the focus was more on commercial success. Publishers and songwriters tried to develop formulas for what was successful. They tended to keep melodies simple.

One writer described the song formula this way: "All their songs had a verse—which could be as short as eight bars, or much longer—and a chorus of eight or sixteen bars. The verses carried the 'action' of the song, and the chorus was repeated after each verse. Usually, the chorus repeated the song's title."[1]

Berlin was a commercial artist. He wanted to write what would have a good chance of selling well. He learned that he had a knack for it. He started experimenting with melodies, common phrases as potential titles, and arrangements. He also wrote about popular subjects like love and employed dialects or street slang, like in his first song "Marie from Sunny Italy." Since he could neither read nor write music, he hired a musical secretary to write it down for him.

Berlin started to become known for his ability to write in dialect. Soon performers came to him to write songs. A vaudeville singer, for example, asked Berlin to write a song about the Italian marathon runner Dorando Pietri.

Berlin decided to do what he did best. He'd make the lyrics funny, use a dialect (Italian), and bring a sweet sadness to the song. It was simple enough for any listener to understand. Berlin presented his song to the vaudeville singer, but he was no longer interested in the song. Dejected, Berlin offered his song to Waterson & Snyder. Waterson listened to the words and was mildly interested. But he wanted to hear the melody before giving further consideration to purchasing the song.

The problem was Berlin had no tune for the song. He had written only the lyrics. Berlin felt his credibility at this important music publisher was on the line. He did not want to look empty-handed. So he bluffed, saying he had written the music.

Waterson then showed Irving Berlin into an office with a piano and blank music sheets. Berlin knew he had to think fast. He would have to make up the music spontaneously. He hummed what came to him, and the arranger jotted down the music without expression. Waterson agreed to pay twenty-five dollars for the song. Not bad, Irving figured, considering the original requestor of the song no longer wanted it.

In April 1909, Berlin, now age twenty-one, wrote another farcical song called "Sadie Salome (Go Home)." It was a funny song about a young upright man who finds his girlfriend is singing in a sexually risqué production. He based the song on a scandalous premier at the Metropolitan Opera of Richard Strauss' *Salome.* The highly controversial production was cancelled after one night. But it lived on in other venues. One of the main actresses took the act to a vaudeville house where audiences liked it.

The song was not a huge hit until it was popularized by Fanny Brice. She was a little-known performer who asked Berlin for a song

A burlesque theater, Minsky's. (Courtesy of Library of Congress, Division of Prints and Photographs)

for her burlesque show. She enlivened the song with self-mockery and physical humor. The song became a success and in many ways helped launch both Berlin's and Brice's careers.

As Fanny sang this song at a burlesque theater, the famed Florenz Ziegfeld took notice of her. He later cast her in his hit *Ziegfeld Follies* of 1910. Her life as an entertainer is depicted in the film *Funny Girl.*

The song got laughs and name recognition for Irving Berlin. But it did not sell many copies of sheet music. Importantly, it led to a change in how Berlin saw himself. He was no longer a singing waiter

Picture of Fanny Brice from the early 1900s before she was cast in Ziegfeld Follies. (Courtesy of Library of Congress, Prints and Photographs Division)

or someone trying to scrap out a tune on a piano. He was a songwriter. Even if his songs didn't sell very well.

Part of the song went:

Sadie Cohen left her happy home
To become an actress lady
On the stage she soon became the rage
As the only real Salomy baby
When she came to town, her sweetheart Mose
Brought for her around a pretty rose
But he got an awful fright
When his Sadie came to sight
He stood up and yelled with all his might:

[Refrain:]

Don't do that dance, I tell you Sadie
That's not a bus'ness for a lady!
'Most ev'rybody knows
That I'm your loving Mose
Oy, Oy, Oy, Oy
Where is your clothes?
You better go and get your dresses
Ev'ryone's got the op'ra glasses
Oy! Such a sad disgrace
No one looks in your face
Sadie Salome, go home

He had a second hit called "That Mesmerizing Mendelssohn Tune" based on the work of Felix Mendelssohn, a German composer, pianist, and conductor who lived in the early-to-mid-1800s. It was a ragtime version of Mendelssohn's "Spring Song" for piano. Berlin explained his enthusiasm for the song. "I had always loved Mendelssohn and his 'Spring Song' and simply wanted to work it into a rag tune." It sold a staggering 500,000 copies of sheet music. With the royalties from this and other songs, Berlin would move his mother and family members into a larger apartment.

With his new self-found responsibility, he would need to find new ideas for songs. He had his eyes and ears out. Sometimes nothing came. Other times, the idea would present itself right before him. For example, one evening he and his friend George Whiting were exchanging banter. Berlin asked Whiting if he was free to attend an event. George smiled and said, "Sure, I'm free. My wife's gone to the country. Hooray!"

That was it. Berlin had found his next song. Borrowing from his friend's phrase, the song was entitled "My Wife's Gone to the Country. Hurrah! Hurrah!" It was funny and something many married men could relate to. Berlin quickly put the words together with George Whiting, and Ted Snyder wrote the tune. The song was a huge hit. Perhaps because the title was simple, catchy, and relatable. It also pushed the boundaries in a subtle yet humorous way on how spouses related to each other. Sales were a whopping 30,000 copies.

Now he was becoming famous. But he still couldn't read or write music. So he hired a trained musician to transcribe the music he composed. He discovered that he could be both the composer and lyricist often by creating simple songs. A biographer described, "A common phrase would come into his head. He used the phrase as a title and wrote a set of lyrics around it."[2] He then conceived a tune at the piano for it. He would tweak the notes until it sounded just right. To give the song flavor, he would often add dialects or street slang. Then, a music transcriber would write it down.

He was developing his own musical style. His songs often told a story in dialect. His songs often named characters making them more personable and real. He stereotyped but usually in an innocuous and comical way.

A contemporary critic of early Irving Berlin songs explains Berlin's technique of writing of songs:

> Berlin's ethnic songs always have a good-natured quality to them that is not necessarily found in songs of this type by other writers . . . He invites the listener to join the character in seeing how ridiculous stereotypes can be. Even though in modern times these songs might be thought to be "politically incorrect," Berlin treats these topics in a manner that is surprisingly lacking in offensiveness.[3]

By now, at twenty-two years old, Berlin was working for Waterson & Snyder. Producers in vaudeville and on Broadway were noticing him. The famous Broadway producers, the Shubert brothers, recruited him to compose musical numbers for their production of *Up and Down Broadway.* It was for this show that Berlin would stumble upon a new, more edgy type of music: ragtime.

Pioneered by Scott Joplin in Missouri, ragtime sprang from the Black community. Rather than a straight melody, ragtime music had a jagged-edge feel to it. This beat was called a syncopated rhythm. Ragtime tunes accented beats that were often unaccented in other musical categories. As one writer put it, "The music was written in a driving rhythm over a strong and steady bass line."[4]

Music goers were accustomed to hearing music at concerts, in restaurants, theaters, or at home in the parlors if a household member played a song on his or her instrument. It was a passive exercise. But ragtime with its pulsating, jagged beat invited the listener to get up and dance. It was exciting.

Some audiences, especially the young, loved the excitement of this music. However, many music publishers, songwriters, and music critics considered ragtime to be "vulgar." Some charged that it invited immorality. Detractors warned that this type of music would encourage

Mural in Arkansas honoring Scott Joplin, the father of ragtime. His music influenced Berlin's composing. (Courtesy Library of Congress, Division of Prints and Photographs)

improper behavior between the sexes. But then this was also the period when short films were first emerging along with nickelodeons. Many condemned those as well. They feared immoral behavior would be encouraged from couples going to a dark room and watching a moving image. Within a decade, many of these critics would be frequently visiting movie houses themselves.

Without his realizing it, Berlin's song in a Broadway show helped remove the stigma of ragtime. Berlin started to write other rags such as the parody "Yiddle on Your Fiddle, Play Some Ragtime." Then, he composed "Alexander and His Clarinet." He later renamed it "Alexander's Ragtime Band."

Scott Joplin is noted as the founder of ragtime music. An African-American composer and pianist, Joplin composed forty-four ragtime pieces as well as one ragtime ballet and two operas which were never performed. His most famous piece is the "Maple Leaf Rag," which is still played today.

Born into a family of railway laborers, Joplin traveled much of the South playing music and eventually settling in St. Louis, Missouri. He taught future ragtime composers and composed music. Sadly, much of his work was not produced during his life. His first opera's score was confiscated for his non-payment of bills. His second opera failed to gain the financial backing to be produced.

He felt cheated out of fame for having developed ragtime music and not being given credit. He also believed Irving Berlin and others had co-opted the musical style he had conceived. After his death at age forty-eight in 1917, ragtime music morphed into jazz emanating from New Orleans and then Chicago and New York City. Later, ragtime's syncopated rhythms spawned big band swing.

About a half-century after his death, his music returned to popularity as featured in the Academy Award winning movie *The Sting*. The film contained a rearranged version of Joplin's "The Entertainer."

Sheet music cover of Berlin's 1909 parody "Yiddle on Your Fiddle, Play Some Ragtime." (Courtesy of Wikimedia Commons)

The tune had no lyrics. But it was catchy. Still, no one was interested in purchasing the song if it was only instrumental. What singer would want it if there was nothing for him or her to sing? A few restaurants played the instrumental-only song for their patrons with little success.

But the song would eventually take on a life of its own.

Now the age of twenty-three, Berlin was invited to a dinner at a famous club for performers and comedians. It was the Friars Club, which is still in operation in midtown Manhattan today, though in a different location. Among the club members were huge stars including George Cohan, one of the most famous songwriters of the day. In receiving the invite, Berlin reflected on his rapid success. Only a few years prior, he was sleeping in flop houses and earning pennies. He was eking out a meager living. Now, he was among some of the best and most famous musicians.

He wanted to show them what he could do. He saw his chance when the club members needed a song for their private comedy show, the *Friars Frolic*. Berlin pulled out his little-known "Alexander's Ragtime Band" and did what he did best—came up with catchy and fun lyrics. The members loved the song.

Soon, the song started to catch on. Musicians started to sing it. Audiences fancied it. Performers were soon playing in multiple venues like restaurants, theaters, and dance halls. Soon after, bands started playing the song in Europe. By the end of 1911, five-and-dime as well as music stores had sold over two million copies of its sheet music.

By the time Berlin was turning twenty-four he had written 200 songs and earned $100,000 in royalties (over two million dollars in today's money). Suddenly his picture appeared on posters. One caption read, "The Composer of a Hundred Hits."

Newspapers pronounced Berlin as the "ragtime king." But he also faced serious opposition. Critics noted that his song was not genuine ragtime. Scott Joplin, the premier composer of ragtime, complained that his music was being co-opted. He asserted that Berlin and other composers stole his ragtime label without properly playing it and without giving him credit. But no one was listening. The world was swept up in the new ragtime beat Berlin had made popular.

Berlin soon became a partner in the music publishing business. His firm was renamed to Waterson, Berlin, & Snyder. But Irving also learned a valuable lesson about his success. He found that many of his colleagues, like Ted Snyder, and fellow songwriters were jealous of his instant fortune. They could not believe that a musically illiterate

An artistic music sheet cover of the popular "That International Rag," published by Watson, Berlin & Snyder. Scott Joplin's genre of ragtime music was becoming mainstream. (Courtesy of Irving Gilmore Music Collection, Yale University)

twenty-three-year-old would make so many hits. They accused him of hiring a Black ragtime pianist to create the melodies and then not giving him any credit. The rumors were untrue.

While Berlin battled these rumors, he encountered another issue. Some of his songs met with resistance from moral reformers. Music lovers all over the world were dancing the turkey trot and other dance crazes to his new hit song "Everybody's Doin It." Sensing their constituency's unease, politicians joined the fray. The mayor of New York City promised to crack down on the music publishers and dance venues promoting these "inappropriate songs."

Despite these controversies, the song had made Berlin wealthy and famous in only his mid-twenties. His days of scraping for change as a newsie and singing waiter were long behind him. He financially helped his mother and several of his siblings. Many of them were still toiling, though, in low-paying sweatshop type jobs. Others were having marital problems.

As a sweet irony, "Alexander's Ragtime Band" became popular in Russia—the land that he had been forced to flee at age five. Now, it was like he was visiting his homeland through his music.

Chapter 5

I Lost the Sunshine and Roses

Berlin was on the rise. One mark of this success was that performers started to ask Berlin if they could perform his songs. One in particular would change Berlin's life. Little-known singer Dorothy Goetz visited his office unexpectedly in 1911. One day, she burst into Berlin's office at Waterson, Berlin & Snyder and pleaded for Berlin to give her one of his tunes to sing for her upcoming act. Boldly, Goetz snatched a music sheet on Berlin's desk and started reading it.

Suddenly, another singer came into the office. She demanded that the song be for her. To Berlin's amazement, Goetz and the other woman began tussling for the sheet music. One punched the other in the face. They kicked and screamed. Berlin finally broke up the fight. The other woman still had the latest song in her hand. She seemed to win the fight.

But Dorothy would win something more lasting. Berlin was intrigued by her energy and confidence. There was something about her that caught his attention. He decided to ask her out on a date. Soon after, Berlin was smitten. After a courtship of just a few months, the two were married in February 1912. They chose Cuba as their honeymoon destination.

Berlin felt like the luckiest man alive. But his good fortune would change in an instant. When the couple returned from their honeymoon, something was very off with Dorothy. She started to show symptoms of typhoid fever. Berlin hired doctors to try to cure her. They tried many methods, but nothing reduced her fever. Her symptoms grew worse. After five months, she died.

Berlin was devastated. The feeling of loss reminded him of his father dying. It also made him think of fleeing from his home country as a small boy. But this was worse—he had not even known his wife for a year. Berlin fell into a depression. He had trouble eating and sleeping.

So he did the only thing he could do: write music. He turned to his

Irving Berlin with his first wife, Dorothy; their marriage would be very short-lived due to her untimely death. (Courtesy of Wikimedia)

trusted piano and composed a sad ballad called "When I Lost You." It was his way of expressing himself. He was turning his sadness into music. He wrote:

> I lost the sunshine and roses.
> I lost the heavens of blue,
> I lost the gladness
> That turned into sadness,
> When I lost you.

For months, Berlin was in a stupor. He grew tired of his job at the music company and wanted to be left alone. Finally, after many months, he was ready to return to the music industry. He wrote the music and lyrics for the musical revue *Stop! Look! Listen!*

A bachelor again, Berlin noticed that the music business was changing. Whereas in decades prior music publishers would take a chance on a little-known composer like Berlin, by 1915 the industry was becoming ultra-competitive and low margin. Typically, a publisher would sell his song for six cents. Of that, the composer would receive one cent. The five cents left over would often go to printing costs, advertising, staff, piano players, and to "pluggers" to sing the songs at cafés. Publishers had to sell more than 300,000 copies of a song just to break even. Some publishers were going out of business.

There was another change afoot. Music composers and publishers grew tired of restaurants and theaters using their songs for free. So they formed a new group that would change the industry forever: ASCAP or the American Society of Composers, Authors (lyricists), and Publishers. They asked cafés, cabarets, and theaters performing their songs to pay for the rights to use them. At first, café owners hesitated, saying the composers should be grateful they were playing their songs at all. But after a court case sided with the composers, the restaurant and café owners gave in. This law change impacted the music industry in a big way. Composers started earning more money.

With this new law in place, Berlin was writing new songs. Yet, he still could not read or write music. He continued to pay music transcribers to jot down what he would hum. Other musicians encouraged Berlin to study music. He tried it for two days. But he quickly gave up, explaining that it was "too tedious." Besides, Berlin protested, while he was studying he could have written more songs.

One of his earliest revues, Berlin's Stop! Look! Listen! *played at the Globe Theater in 1915 with the book by Harry Smith.* (Courtesy of Wikimedia Commons)

He felt ready for a change. He had great success in writing hit songs. Yet he did not have control over their publication. Why not, he thought, try to start his own business.

And so he took the plunge. Irving Berlin, Inc. was born. Max Winslow became his partner. The two moved uptown to the budding theater district. Berlin figured that moving to this location would allow him to be closer to the beat of Broadway. He could figure out the best ways to pitch his music to producers.

Chapter 6

How I Hate to Get Up in the Morning

By this time, World War I or the Great War, as it was known, had broken out in Europe. The US had managed to stay out of the war for the initial three years. Berlin supported staying out of the war. One of the most popular songs of the day was "I Didn't Raise My Boy to Be a Soldier." It encapsulated how many felt about the raging war: that it was Europe's issue. Americans watched on news reels and read in newspapers about the bloodshed happening in Germany, France, and Britain. Soldiers were dug in among trenches. Many were getting hit with machine gun fire and sustaining painful and life-altering injuries. Sadly, the war was the first to use chemical warfare. Soldiers were literally being gassed to death. The goal of the war was unclear even to the fighting soldiers. American asked themselves, "Why should the US intervene and put its treasury and soldiers' blood on the line?" The US stayed out of the gruesome war.

But by 1917, times were different. German U-boats were blocking American ships. The Germans also sank the *Lusitania* causing passengers, including Americans, to drown. These events contributed to President Woodrow Wilson's about-face on US intervention. He declared that the US must "make the world safe for democracy." A patriotic sentiment swept the nation as it coped with war. Berlin's mentor George Cohan penned one of his most famous songs "Over There" about Allied victory. The most famous verse was:

Over there, over there
Send the word, send the word over there
That the Yanks are coming
The Yanks are coming
The drums rum-tumming
Everywhere

Suddenly, American culture was anti-German. Sauerkraut was renamed liberty cabbage. Schools stopped teaching German. Friends encouraged Berlin to change his last name to something less German sounding. Berlin shrugged off their suggestion.

A statue of iconic composer George Cohan, known for his patriotic tunes like "Over There," stands at the heart of Times Square. He was a mentor for Berlin and may have served as an early inspiration for the song that would eventually become "God Bless America." (Courtesy Wikimedia, photo by Steven Lek.)

Berlin caught some of the patriotic fervor that simmered across the US in 1917. Sensing the shift in tone, he composed the patriotic hit song "For Your Country and My Country." The song would be used for war recruiting efforts.

He decided to become a US citizen. He took the formal oath and it was official. The honeymoon was short-lived, however. Within a few weeks he was drafted into the army. Suddenly, the war became personal.

He reluctantly set off for Camp Upton in Yaphank, Long Island, about seventy miles east of Manhattan. Troops at the camp expected to be shipped out to France after completing training. There was no guarantee they would ever come back alive.

Army life was hard but not nearly as difficult as the life he had once lived on Cherry Street. It was nothing compared to the harsh labor conditions that many of his siblings still toiled in. But that was all behind Berlin. He had gotten used to being famous and living comfortably, having made a lot of money from his song royalites. He was said to have arrived to the rustic army base by a chauffered limousine from Manhattan. If true, it seemed inappropriate to the other soldiers. He exchanged his more fashionable clothes for a uniform, helmut, and a gun with a bayonet.

Now, in the army, he was just another soldier. He was required to sleep in a long, nondescript barrack with, according to his song, ninety-seven men. He was no longer socializing with Broadway stars or staying up late to write a song that popped into his head. Now, he was marching, following barked orders from commanders, and performing drills. The work was routine. But the worst part for him was having to get up early in the morning.

It did not take long for Berlin to realize that he was not cut out for the army. Despite his efforts, he continued to have trouble getting up so early every day. But he tried to fit in. He later recounted, "Every morning when the bugle blew in the Reveille, I'd jump right out of bed as if I liked getting up early. The other soldiers thought I was a little too eager about it, and they hated me."[1]

So Berlin did what he knew best. He wrote a song about it. It was fittingly titled "Oh! How I Hate to Get Up in the Morning." In the song, he dreams of murdering the bugler, who sounded the musical alarm every morning to get up, so he can "spend the rest of his life in bed."

His song had the refrain:

Irving Berlin sings his parody "How I Hate to Get Up in the Morning" while stationed at Camp Yaphank in Upton, Long Island, New York. (Courtesy of the Library of Congress, Division of Prints and Photographs, New York World Telegram and Sun Collection)

You've got to get up,
you've got to get up,
you've got to get up this morning!

Like many of Berlin's songs, the tune was simple and the lyrics were easily understandable. Anyone could relate to the song, making it popular. As with many of his previous songs, he employed the local dialect and language. In this case, that was using phrases commonly used on an army base.

Irving Berlin is drafted into the army once the US enters World War I. He composed the famed "How I Hate to Get Up in the Morning" while stationed at Camp Yaphank in Upton, Long Island, New York. (Courtesy of Wikimedia Commons)

Berlin was pleased soldiers and civilians liked his song. But his song didn't solve the problem of having to get up early. Then, soldier Berlin saw his chance. The camp's commander, General Bell, was looking to raise money for a visitor's center. He called Berlin into his office.

Bell looked over the musician-turned-soldier and wondered if Berlin could help. He spoke with candor and a bit of uncertainty that was unusual for a general.

"We want a place where friends and relatives of the men can be made a little more comfortable when they come to visit. It could cost a lot of money—perhaps $35,000 and we thought perhaps you could put on a little show to make that money."

Berlin was taken aback. He hadn't expected such an offer. He had been getting used to being "just another soldier." He thought of many of the entertainers he had met at the camp. Since Camp Upton was only about seventy miles from New York City, the entertainment capital of the US at the time, it was not surprising. "Do you know how many people in this Army are from show business? The camp is full of them. Fine actors, vaudeville headliners, acrobats, singers. Why don't we put on a show with these people? We could even play it on Broadway to boost morale, help recruiting, everything!"[2] Used to pitching music publishers, Berlin popped his pressing question. "Here's the thing, General. I write at night. And I couldn't do that if I had to get up in the morning at five, you understand."

"Why, you don't have to get up at five AM. You just forget about all

A music sheet cover for the famous song that Berlin wrote while stationed at Camp Yaphank in Long Island, New York. He was never a morning person. (Courtesy of Irving S. Gilmore Music Library, Yale University)

that. You write this show," the general exclaimed.[3] Berlin had scored twice. Now, he could return to writing music instead of doing mundane soldier tasks all day. And he could sleep in. But he still needed a quiet room and a piano to work. How could he be creative amidst the hustle-and-bustle of the camp? The general acquiesced to this request as well.

Irving Berlin at the piano. He taught himself to play and never studied music formally. (Courtesy of the Library of Congress, Division of Prints and Photographs, New York World Telegram and Sun Collection)

He decided to write a collection of songs and humorous scenes rather than a show with one narrative and plot. He tinkered with a few ideas for skits, sometimes drawing on what he had observed at the camp. He eventually came up with *Yip Yip Yaphank*, the first wartime musical comedy.

The show was a hodge podge of marching drills, jugglers, acrobats—all in uniform. Performers danced in chorus lines, played in comedy sketches, and sang tunes. What made the show funny was that it was all performed by soldiers. Most were not professional actors. So the audience would catch some notes sung off-key or almost-missed lines. It was amateur but in an authentic way.

Berlin also wanted to add some patriotic music. This was the army after all. So Berlin came up with "God Bless America." It was a sentimental song about the composer's newfound homeland. He felt a pride in being American and expressed it through the lyrics.

But upon further reflection he found the song too sappy, overly sentimental. Besides, it was redundant to many of the show's other songs. So he dropped it from the program. Little did he know that within two decades it would become one of the most famous and patriotic songs ever written.

Audiences loved the show. They were entertained and moved. It took their minds off the seriousness of the war. It poked fun at army life—where everything was often taken so seriously. Stars of the day including Al Jolson, Eddie Cantor, Fanny Brice, and Will Rogers attended performances. They liked the show and recommended it for a limited run in New York's theater district.

Also pleased with the show, General Bell decided to move performances to the Century Theatre in New York. There, the theater could hold thousands so the Camp could raise far more money.

About three hundred military men in full battle gear were to perform the show nightly at the Century Theatre. The show was advertised as "A Military Musical 'Mess' Cooked Up By the Boys at Camp Upton." The soldiers were stationed at the 71st Regiment Armory on Park Avenue and 34th Street. (The building there remains the Armory to the present day). For each performance, to drum up enthusiasm they would march up Park Avenue, bear west on the famed 42nd Street, and then head north up Eighth Avenue to the Century Theatre at 62nd Street.

Opening night was August 19, 1918. Tickets were sold out. The soldiers were nervous backstage. They had not imagined they would be performing in a major theater when they signed up or were drafted into the army.

The performance began with a minstrel show where some performing soldiers donned blackface. By today's standards, blackface is completely unacceptable and was cruel in its mockery of African-Americans. But by the values of the day, it was totally accepted and rather popular entertainment. That segment was followed by a vaudeville segment with jugglers, acrobats, and other circus-like acts. Then, there were revues of "girls" who were actually male soldiers dressed up as women. Irving sang his beloved "Oh! How I Hate to Get Up in the Morning" production. Stage stars and producers were in the audience to support the effort.

Yip Yip Yaphank was a box office smash. The show extended from eight to thirty-two performances and made $83,000 (about $1.4 million in today's money) for Camp Upton.

General Bell was also delighted. After the opening night performance, he addressed the audience: "I have heard that Berlin is among the foremost songwriters of the world, and now I believe it... Berlin is as good a soldier as he is a songwriter, and as popular in Camp Upton as he is on Broadway."[4] Not bad for a soldier who felt he was a total misfit for the army.

Then, the final performance came. On stage, there was an unusual tension in the air. It was not only because this was the last show. It was going to be the last time some of the performers would be in the US. They were about to enter into harm's way on the battlefield.

At the show's finale, the company marched off the stage, and the audience cheered. Yet, somehow their cheers were dimmed as the soldiers marched in formation. The audience was bewildered. They suddenly realized that the cast had exited the theater to march off to war. They would now leave their base to prepare to be dispatched to Europe. Within a month, they would make their journey overseas to the dangerous battlefields of Europe.

As the soldiers marched off into the night, the audience was stunned as the story performed on stage became real. Audience members who were loved ones of the soldier-actors had no idea if and when they'd ever see them again. It was a moment where the humor of the show and the songs stopped. Reality had set in.

Chapter 7

Music in the 1920s

When the war ended in 1918, like every other soldier, Berlin returned to civilian life. He returned to his own firm, Irving Berlin, Inc. His business was to record, market, and distribute all his songs plus those from other composers and lyricists. Yet the world was a different place than it had been before he left to join the army.

His home country of Russia had changed forever with the Russian Revolution in late 1917. Berlin had sometimes used headlines for songs. The Bolshevik overthrow of the Czarist Russian government inspired him to compose "That Revolutionary Rag." He then took the song to Max Dreyfus, the chief of the prominent T.B. Harms music publishing company. Dreyfus thought well of the song and requested that his staff composer take notations. That composer would become one of the most important songwriters of the twentieth century. It was none other than George Gershwin, who was not yet famous.

Gershwin and Berlin had met two years prior for a similar productive yet unmemorable meeting about another song. Berlin did not remember the meeting. The two soon-to-be world-class composers revamped the song. Berlin joked, "The [resulting] song was so good I didn't recognize it." The tune ended up having more of a jazz beat than a ragtime one. Perhaps without realizing it, Berlin and Gershwin were adapting their music to changing times—the coming of the Jazz Age.

The change in music was one of many transformations Berlin observed in 1920. For thirty years, the Progressive Era had ushered in many sweeping social and political reforms, like women's suffrage, housing improvement laws, the personal income tax, and worker protections.

Moreover, Prohibition had been enacted after a hard fought battle from an unlikely alliance of Protestant ministers and social reformers. Alcohol had played a major role in socializing, whether at home or in restaurants, bars, or saloons. Now, serving alcohol continued but underground in speakeasies. It was also in 1920 that the federal constitutional amendment for women's suffrage had been ratified. In New York, the women's right to vote had passed by referendum only a few years prior. Suddenly, women had much more of a voice in political decisions.

Labor unions had also made much progress. Berlin's siblings had worked countless hours toiling away in sweatshops making garments and rolling cigars. Many of the children Berlin grew up with were essentially forced to work at a young age. They had few rights. Berlin himself had struggled as a newsie. He and his fellow newsies were exploited by the newspaper publishers who employed them. Since Berlin's teenage years though, the public had become more sympathetic to the needs of labor. Unions began taking on more members and demanding certain rights.

Perhaps one of the most important sociological changes during this time was the rise of the middle class. When Berlin and his family arrived in New York City there was the very rich and the poor. There were

Women march for the right to vote. While some states enacted the law, it was not until 1920 that the US constitutional amendment was ratified. (Courtesy of Library of Congress, Department of Prints and Photographs)

few in between. But from economic growth, the middle class emerged. Maybe one of the most important symbols of the middle class was the piano. Many families had made the investment to purchase and take lessons on the piano. It was a way to hear music at home in an age before recorded music or the radio.

But now the Progressive Era was giving way to the Roaring Twenties. The public was turning away from government intervention and social reform. Overblown fears of communism swept the land, and government policies were changing. The Immigration Act of 1924 dramatically slowed the tide of immigrants to the US. Had Moses Baline, Irving's father, tried to enter the US at that point, he likely would have been denied. An anti-communism fervor prevailed. It's likely that Berlin would have seen socialist protest and anti-protestors. For instance, he would have heard about the infamous explosion on Wall Street on September 16, 1920, by anarchists which killed forty and injured hundreds.

The *Brooklyn Daily Eagle* headline read: "Scores Die; 200 Hurt in Wall St. Explosion; Cause a Mystery; Morgan Bank Wrecked."[1]

These events likely shaped his own world perceptions and his songwriting.

Under Presidents Warren Harding and Calvin Coolidge, the US had turned more conservative, partly as a reaction to anarchist rioters. Less government, more big business was the new sentiment. The stock market was booming, and Americans were feeling good again. They were spending money and looking for fun times. New dance crazes like the Charleston and turkey trot swept the nation. Music reflected these new patterns—the Jazz Age described as "ragtime music loosened up" became the rage in New York City's Harlem music clubs. Big band music started to become popular as well.

But as one trend rises, another dims. Tin Pan Alley's music, which once captivated many homes with its sheet music of comical or enchanting music, was no longer as popular. Ragtime, comic dialect songs, and love ballads had fallen out of favor. In this post-Victorian era, some Americans were jettisoning what they saw as traditional conservative values. An evolving middle class meant more had disposable income. Young single women were working for the first time, pocketing some of their leftover paychecks. These new social classes and economic opportunities gave rise to freer kinds of music—which many Americans deemed as risqué and lacking of morals. As one example, a newspaper article headline read, "Moral Letdown Heritage of Jazz Age, Says Reformer." Berlin would need to adjust his musical style once again.

Tin Pan Alley faced not only declining consumer demand but also significant competition from both recorded music and piano rolls. This new musical invention of piano rolls enabled the piano to play a tune by itself. No longer did someone have to purchase sheet music and be schooled in playing the piano to enjoy the tune. People also started buying phonograph records at a higher rate than sheet music. Tin Pan Alley executives feared their customers would stop singing from—and buying—sheet music once they were in the habit of listening to recorded music.

Their fears were founded in Berlin's new song *You'd Be Surprised.* The recorded song stunned music executives when it sold 800,000 copies, outpacing its sheet music sales. Other hit songs at the time sold on average 150,000 piano rolls and 1.2 million phonograph records

Cartoon is a parody of Tin Pan Alley. The caption reads, "Crazy! Him? That's th' slickest bimbo in th' place. Just busts phonograph records t' pieces, glues 'em t'gether again an' turns out ten new jazz hits a day!" The depiction implies that Tin Pan Alley had become a factory for manufacturing popular, but not necessarily well-produced, music. (Courtesy of the Library of Congress, Division of Prints and Photographs)

with a comparatively small one million copies of sheet music. These new forms of music were eclipsing sheet music sales.[2]

Then, another technological innovation would transform the popular music business forever—the radio. By 1921, radios were broadcasting church services, concerts, sporting events, and music to national audiences. Newspapers exclaimed, "There is radio music in the air, every night, everywhere. Anybody can hear it at home on a receiving set, which any boy can put up in an hour."[3]

At first, music publishers resisted letting their songs play for free on the radio but soon realized that radios had to pay royalties to songwriters and song publishers. Consequently, radios became the new way to advertise new songs, and buskers and pluggers were no longer needed. Berlin's former profession of busking was on its way out.

Amidst these sweeping changes, Berlin and his company wanted to stay on top of the latest music trends. The "ragtime king" had to reinvent himself. Berlin confessed not to understand exactly what jazz was. But then he had said the same of ragtime a decade prior. That did not stop him from composing songs in those genres.

Berlin was a quintessential commercial composer. He wrote songs that he believed would be popular and make substantial profits in sales not necessarily pieces that would advance the art. He saw himself as a business person as much as a composer. He looked for formulas in writing songs that would make them appealing. He'd need to reinvent those formulas.

Always the commercial songwriter, he kept tabs on what the public was buying. For example, he commented that the public was more interested in sad songs than happy ones. He admitted, "It has always been assumed that whenever I've written a ballad, I've been through some heartbreaking experience. But the real reason is that the public would rather buy tears than smiles—and right now they happen to want sob ballads."[4]

Chapter 8

A Theater of His Own

Florenz Ziegfeld was one of the splashiest and most groundbreaking showmen of the early 1920s. He was raised in a more classical music tradition, but he veered towards the crowd-pleasing visually beautiful shows. Actor William Powell, who later played him in *The Great Ziegfeld*, described "his love for show business, his exquisite taste, his admiration for the beauty of women. He was financially impractical but aesthetically impeccable—a genius in his chosen field."[1] Thinking out of the box, Ziegfeld produced some of the first colorful and visually spectacular musicals with elaborate costumes and sets.

Around 1920, he was working on his new theatrical spectacular *Ziegfeld Follies* for which he'd need a score. He asked Berlin to write it. Berlin had written ragtime music (though some claim that music was not the "real ragtime") and lots of funny, sad, or farcical songs, but he hadn't written an entire musical before. He was not exactly sure how, but that had never stopped him before. He agreed.

Ziegfeld wanted Berlin to write "Ziegfeld Girl numbers" in order to "showcase the showgirls." He wrote two tunes that really caught on with the audience, "A Pretty Girl Is Like a Melody" and "You'd Be Surprised." Berlin first observed the costumes the showgirls would be wearing and then wrote the sequence around that theme. The soundtrack sold eight hundred thousand copies.

"A Pretty Girl Is Like a Melody" has a slow, steady rhythm which allows the beautiful women dancers to walk in unison with their elaborate costumes. To a modern eye, the scene looked almost like a fashion show. Singer John Steel starts the refrain with "A pretty girl is like a melody/that haunts you night and day." Musicologists note that subsequent verses from this show follow pattern lyrics that mimic classical tunes.

Though Berlin had no musical education, he was well-versed in classical pieces. For this number, he used Antonin Dvorak's

Photo from 1936 film The Great Ziegfeld, *which artfully depicts Florenz Ziegfeld Jr.'s rise to a famed musical producer. The film showcases elaborate numbers from his iconic* Ziegfeld Follies. *Fanny Brice made an appearance as herself in the film.* (Courtesy of Wikimedia)

"Humoresque" and Felix Mendelssohn's "Spring Song" among others. Berlin used the song not only for the theme of this show but its rhythmic pattern for later works too. Due to its popularity, this musical format became the template for similar numbers in many musical revues of subsequent decades. Berlin later would credit the tune as "the best individual song written for a musical."[2] Audiences loved the song and the visual spectacular that followed it. Its scene was dramatically portrayed in the 1936 MGM film *The Great Ziegfeld.*

A music sheet cover for the 1927 Ziegfeld Follies *showcasing showgirls, popular comedian Eddie Cantor, and produced by Irving Berlin, Inc.* (Courtesy of Irving Gilmore Music Library, Yale University)

Music Box

His songs were popular but Berlin had bigger ideas. He thought of becoming a producer or partnering with one. He didn't like being a "hired hand" of shows who wrote on order. He forged a friendship with Sam Harris, a prominent Broadway producer. Harris wanted to have his own theater to control the creative content on shows—sets, costumes, scripts etc.—and to focus on musicals. Best of all,

Harris figured, he would own the theater and not have to pay rent to a commercial landlord. Harris understood that one of producers' largest expenses was often not actors' or musicians' salaries but the theater rent.

Harris knew the business of running a theater but he didn't have much artistic talent. For that, he turned to Berlin to partner with him. An entrepreneur at heart, Berlin loved the idea. He and Harris decided to call their theater "The Music Box." Located on 45th Street and Broadway just three blocks from bustling Times Square, the new theater was to showcase Berlin's musicals. The duo hired architect C. Howard Crane to build a theater in neo-Georgian style with two vertical sides separated by classical columns, shudders in windows, and rounded arches on the top. The interior was ornate with gold décor, crafted water fountains, velvet-covered seats, wood trims, and chandeliers hanging from the ceiling. Though the theater was not large by modern standards, its craftsmanship inside would create a premium experience for the theatergoer. New York City architecture at the time, whether train stations, banks, or theaters, was about creating inspiration and an experience. Classical architecture was in vogue. (The same theater still stands and houses smash hits like *Dear Evan Hansen* and famed revivals including *Cat on a Hot Tin Roof* and *Pippin.*)

Harris and Berlin had the vision for their new theater—but not the cash to fund it. So they turned to Joseph Schenck, known as more of a movie mogul with 20th Century Pictures (later Twentieth Century Fox and currently Twentieth Century Studios), to finance the construction. He was made a partner. So with the theater built, Berlin set off to write the *Music Box Revue.* He composed what would become its most famous song—"Say It with Music"—which would become the theme song of Berlin's later Music Box Revues. It is a romantic song about the language of love being told through music. The second verse goes: "There's a tender message deep down in my heart/Something you should know, but how am I to start? Sentimental speeches never could impart/Just exactly what I want to tell you." Though a bit sappy by modern standards, the song struck a chord with listeners.

Partly from this song, the show was a thundering success. Critics raved, and the house was full for almost every performance. The producers made profits from ticket sales and the sheet music that patrons would buy after hearing the music on stage. They also released the show music as an album. That was somewhat of a novelty. From these multiple revenue sources, Berlin and his partner were able to pay back all of Schenck's investment.

With this success, Berlin and his team produced new shows each year. Berlin recruited leading performers of the day including Fanny Brice and the Brox Sisters. These shows would compete head-on with *Ziegfeld's Follies* along with other revues such as *Scandals* from fellow composer George Gershwin. The Music Box was pioneering in that never before had a songwriter or director built the theater in which their works were performed. The undertaking was a huge financial risk. But it paid off.

By the early 1920s, Berlin had a newfound confidence. He was leaving behind his Yiddish-sounding songs and parodies in favor of songs that would work on a Broadway stage for larger audiences. With his commercial success, Berlin was *setting* the standard for popular music rather than always *following* it. He experimented with musical form and the use of language. But he composed fewer ethnic songs with dialects. He was becoming mainstream—with its benefits and its trappings of conventionality.

Photo of operetta composer Victor Herbert, Irving Berlin, and "march king" John Philip Sousa in 1924. (Courtesy of the Library of Congress, Prints and Photographs Division)

Actors walk outside the Music Box that Irving Berlin co-founded. (Courtesy of the Library of Congress, Prints and Photographs Division, Library of Congress, New York World-Telegram & Sun Collection)

Berlin would personally feel some of the sentiments expressed in his songs. In the summer of 1922, his mother passed away. She had lived in the US for about three decades but had never really assimilated into American culture. Soon after, his old friend Mike Salter, who ran the Pelham Café where Berlin got his start, died as well.

Chapter 9

Ellin Mackay

Saddened by these losses, Berlin attended a dinner gathering to forget his troubles for a while. Little did he know that this evening would change the rest of his life. Unexpectedly, he met the socialite Ellin Mackay, who came from one of the wealthiest families at the time in the US.

She charmed him by saying, "Oh, Mr. Berlin, I do so like your song, 'What Shall I Do?'" He thanked her for the compliment but noted that she was indirectly referencing his mistaken grammar in the title confusing "will" and "shall." He responded, "Where grammar is concerned, I can always use a little help."

After dinner, he invited her to accompany him to Jimmy Kelly's, where he once worked. Since Prohibition began in 1919, the venue had become a speakeasy, serving alcohol illicitly. Jim Kelly's had also moved from his old Union Square location to Sullivan Street in Greenwich Village. That area was becoming known for its social protests and artistic experimentation.

Berlin had heard of Ellin Mackay. Most had—her background was legendary. Her father, Clarence Mackay, who inherited his family's fortune in the Nevada Comstock silver mines, was one of New York's wealthiest men. He owned the highly successful Postal Telegraph Company. He built a mansion on Long Island with fifty rooms and employed one hundred servants. She attended the best schools and danced with the Prince of Wales.

In a way, her and Berlin's meeting was indicative of the vast social changes that had recently occurred. Only a few decades prior, it would have been very rare for a young woman of such stature to socialize with anyone outside her class. But social classes began to break down with the cabarets in 1910. Young girls from the highest echelons of society would be in the same audience as men from lower and even immigrant classes. The ideal of a woman was being transformed. The embodiment of that became the Jazz Age flapper—a 1920s fashionable young woman.

Amidst these changes, Ellin longed for a more literary life outside the confines of her strict social class upbringing. She was drawn to the Algonquin Round Table, a group of legendary figures such as Dorothy Parker. She wrote for a new magazine, which ultimately would become one of the most prestigious in the country, *The New Yorker*. One of her first pieces was about this phenomenon of the breakdown of social classes called "Why We Go to Cabarets: A Post-Debutante Explains."

She and Berlin dated for months. They went to shows and silent films. Not long after, Berlin proposed marriage. But Ellin's father vehemently opposed their relationship. He objected to his high-class

Irving with his new spouse, Ellin Mackay. She was the daughter of one of the wealthiest men in the US at the time, who greatly disapproved of their relationship. (Courtesy of Wikipedia Commons)

daughter marrying a Jewish songwriter and an immigrant. Years earlier, his wife had left him for a prominent society surgeon. So Clarence was especially wary of any romantic intention involving anyone in his family.

He hired private detectives to find "dirt" on Berlin. They came up with nothing. So her father sent her off to Europe so that she would forget about him.

Artistic music sheet cover of the popular Music Box Revue *from 1922-23.* (Courtesy of Irving S. Gilmore Music Library, Yale University)

But the opposite happened. With Ellin away, Berlin grew even fonder of her. He wrote favorite songs like "What'll I Do?" and "All Alone" to express his loneliness. Missing Ellin, he also composed a song called "Remember."

As Berlin struggled to maintain his relationship with Ellin, his *Music Box Revue* started to falter—along with his confidence. The show continued to garner positive critical reviews, but ticket sales slowed. For the first time, Berlin started losing money. It became apparent that audiences wanted something different. At the same time, he played his new songs on the piano and sang lyrics for his publishing associates. But they were not enthusiastic about the songs and were concerned that audiences wouldn't respond well to them. They tried to dissuade Berlin from publishing it. The rejection devastated Berlin. He recounted his experience:

> On Christmas morning, I called Max Winslow and Saul Bornstein, my publishing associates, to my studio room in the Music Box Theatre to hear the new song I had composed. I sang it, certain I had a hit. When I finished . . . Bornstein said that it was not so good. Winslow said it was terrible. I told them I thought the song was good and would be a hit. They suggested I throw it into the wastebasket and forget about it . . . I thought I had lost my skill, my talent. I was afraid to write anything for fear Winslow would say it was terrible. I was developing an inferiority complex, which is the greatest hindrance a writer can have. I worried so much that I was becoming a bundle of nerves. That Christmas Day was the worst one I had ever spent in my life. Every time I felt worried or troubled I remembered that day and felt worse.[1]

He wondered whether he'd ever write a great song again.

Losing money and tired of having to turn out a yearly revue score, Berlin wanted to end the show's run. His inspiration for composing original songs was diminishing. He also thought that renting out the theater space to another production would probably be as profitable as producing his own. So he closed the show for good in 1924.

The music scene was continuing to change. Patrons were seeing silent films instead of going to the theater for entertainment. They listened to the radio and frequented movie theaters, as they were more affordable and convenient. In living rooms across the US, families gathered around radios to listen to broadcasts, comedy acts, and a variety of music. Listeners were introduced to a wider range of music from folk to jazz. The way Berlin composed songs was out of step with the Roaring Twenties.

Jazz became a standard attraction in bars and dance halls. Skilled musicians were using marches, popular songs, and ragtime tunes to improvise, or create new melodies on the spot. Unlike with classical music, the casual player could not just purchase sheet music and easily play jazz at home. So music sheet publishers, including Berlin's old firm Waterson, Berlin & Snyder, were faltering.

As he dealt with financial matters and regaining his footing in the music business, he also tried to reignite his romantic relationship with Ellin. She returned to New York after a year. The media covered their romance with sensationalized headlines for their nosy readers. But Ellin's father, Clarence Mackay, vowed the two would never marry. "Over my dead body," he said.

But the couple eloped and married without his knowledge in early 1926. Mackay's office workers told Clarence of the wedding. It became obvious. The phones at the Postal Telegraph Company were ringing incessantly. Reporters were calling him for his reaction. He told them he had not consented to the marriage. He also wrote her out of his will. Her share had been estimated at ten million dollars.

Reporters mobbed the couple. It was an irresistible story. They knew their readers would be fascinated by the scandal and therefore purchase their newspapers or magazines. That way, their papers could increase revenues not only from more copies sold but also from increased rates to advertisers. Some reporters claimed that their marriage was a publicity stunt to promote Berlin's songs. The two escaped to a honeymoon in Europe. Berlin celebrated their marriage by writing one of his most memorable songs, "Always."

Clarence was unrelenting in his disapproval of the couple. Eventually, through a series of talks, Berlin offered her father two million dollars. That seemed to do the trick. His feelings of indignation subsided.

Talkies: Films with Sound

As Berlin was celebrating his marriage, he realized that film was going to change as significantly as music had just a decade before with the advent of radio. In 1927, film studio Warner Brothers changed movies forever with the introduction of "talkies." From the first feature-length film *Birth of a Nation* in 1915 to this point, all pictures were silent. Moviegoers read subtitles, and often a live piano player provided musical accompaniment.

In the mid-1920s, the studio pioneered the use of the Vitaphone, which picked up actors' voices. The innovation was also an attempt of the Warner brothers, Harry, Albert, Sam, and Jack, to turn around their fledgling company. The Vitaphone was a primitive system that synchronized film using a disc. It was passable for "shorts" but not for feature-length films.

The first "talkie" was *The Jazz Singer*, which depicted a cantor's son who chooses show business over his synagogue to use his musical talents for entertainment purposes. Most of the film is silent, though, except for the singing.

Al Jolson sang six songs on the Vitaphone soundtrack for *The Jazz Singer*, each synchronized to his image on screen. The songs had little connection to the plot, but producers liked when performers sang popular songs in films though because it was likely to boost a film's fame.

As the film planning progressed, producers decided to include Berlin's recent hit "Blue Skies." This would be included in the scene where Jolson returns home to share stories of his show business success with his mother. The scene echoed Berlin's life as the son of a cantor who later financially assists his mother. By contemporary standards, the scene appears stilted and canned. But audiences would have been so wowed by characters speaking that the scene's content is secondary.

With the success of *The Jazz Singer*, Hollywood began making "talkies," or pictures with sound, by the dozen. The first all-talkie was the American crime drama *Lights of New York*, released a year later. The Warner Brothers rights to this innovative equipment was short-lived. By 1928, the Warners no longer enjoyed exclusivity to sound. Other motion picture studios raced to make talkies. One problem though was that some movie theaters were slow to adopt the new technology. Some film executives believed talkies were a "flash in the pan" and would not be favored long-term by audiences. Consequently, investing in these technologies, they reasoned, would be foolhardy. They were wrong.

As part of this transition, Hollywood film studios bought many of the music publishers on Tin Pan Alley. The studios then owned all the rights to their songs. Soon, almost all popular songs were coming from Hollywood rather than from Tin Pan Alley. Berlin, though, refused to sell his music publishing company. His company was one of the last holdouts. But Berlin knew that he had to turn his talents and attention to Hollywood. So he opened an office there.

Berlin found creating numbers for movies easier than for musical comedies. Film scores could be simple songs. But musical theater songs

The back of a music sheet features the hit song "Blue Skies." The ad also reminds consumers that the "Number can also be had for your Phonograph and Player Piano." (Courtesy of Irving Gilmore Music Library, Yale University)

often had to tie into the plot. As Berlin wrote new musicals, he struck up a friendship with a fellow songwriter of his age—Cole Porter. The two were the only major songwriters of the day who wrote both their own music and lyrics. Cole Porter had trouble breaking into show business. His music was often seen as too sophisticated for both theater and film audiences. The two formed a mutually beneficial friendship. Berlin offered the music simplicity that audiences tended to like. He also supported Porter's efforts by paying for advertising for his shows. Porter, on the other hand, with his Yale and Harvard education, exhibited that educational sophistication in music that Berlin never had.

Berlin would later become an admirer of Porter's work. In a letter to Porter in 1933 upon the release of the popular song "Night and Day," Berlin wrote:

> I am mad about "Night and Day," and I think it is your high spot. You probably know it is being played all over, all the orchestra leaders think it is the best tune of the year—and I agree with them. Really, Cole, it is great. I could not resist the temptation of writing you about it.
> Love from us to you and Linda.[2]

Berlin's warm affection would continue decades later with the opening one of Cole Porter's most famous works *Kiss Me, Kate.* He wrote in a Western Union telegram dated January 4, 1949, to the Waldorf Astoria in New York City where Porter was staying:

> Ellin [Berlin's wife] and I saw Kiss Me Kate last night and thought it was swell. Congratulations on a wonderful job and a smash. Let's see you soon so I can tell you in person what I think of the many high spots.
> Love, Irving.[3]

Berlin Works in Film

Berlin's entrance to writing for film started around 1924. Playwright and humorist George Kaufman and Berlin signed on to the chaotic project of writing and composing a play for the Marx Brothers. They were the famed slapstick foursome of Groucho, Chico, Harpo, and Zeppo. Berlin was reluctant, though he had the time. Sam Harris convinced him to take on the project. Harris explained it was a unique opportunity to write songs for the "town's hottest new comedy team."

The show, entitled *The Cocoanuts*, parodied the mid-1920s real estate boom in South Florida. Not long after the draining of Miami Beach in 1915, prospectors, speculators, and nearby residents flocked to the area bidding up prices. It also invited scammers, who are portrayed in the film as fraudulent auctioneers driving up the land values. Get-rich-quick schemes shot the market up.

Anecdotes were that lots that had sold for $800 in 1920 were selling for $150,000 in 1924. Some lots were advertised as "outside Miami Beach." In reality, they were quite outside—by about 70 miles. This wackiness was ripe for satire. (Little did they know when they wrote the show that in two years, the bubble would burst. Those who had bought too late were unable to sell the properties. Then, the Great Hurricane of 1926 devastated the area.)

Photo of Cole Porter, a contemporary of Irving Berlin best known for musicals like Kiss Me, Kate *and* Anything Goes. (Courtesy Library of Congress, Department of Prints and Photographs)

So Berlin joined Kaufman in writing for the new Marx Brothers show. The two stayed in adjoining in rooms in a hotel during the creative writing process. Berlin would occasionally burst in with a new song he had drafted. He was always very sensitive to feedback and if someone didn't like his song, he sometimes would discard it. Kaufman described this phenomenon in the *New Yorker:*

> About the second week, Irving woke me up at five o'clock one morning to sing me a song he had just finished. Now, Irving has a pure but hardly strong voice, and since I am not very strong myself at 5 am,

> I could not catch a word of it. Moving to the edge of my bed, he sat down and sang it again, and again. I failed to get it. Just when it looked as though he would have to get into my bed before I could hear it, he managed, on the third try, to put it across.[4]

Kaufman did like the song and put it in the show. Despite lots of drama and chaos in the rehearsals, the show opened on December 8, 1925 at the Lyric. It opened to favorable reviews and box office success. Theater critic Percy Hammond for the *New York Herald Tribune* observed,

> The Cocoanuts was large and unpretentious, and was built on the usual specifications. Mr. Irving Berlin made himself heard in a suburban melodee [sic], entitled A Little Bungalow, and Mr. Kaufman, the author, delivered a dotty fable concerning Florida real estate, a stolen necklace and a love affair between a hotel clerk and a soprano heiress. A brilliant, eleven dollar audience rejoiced. The major Marx is one of those gifted clowns who can make good jokes out of bad ones.[5]

Groucho Marx improvised during the show. Sometimes, he unexpectedly interacted with audience members. As one example, during one show, Groucho saw President Calvin Coolidge in his box in the audience. He inquired of the president, "Isn't it a little past your bedtime, Cal?"

With the show's success, the producers agreed to finance a film a few years later with Berlin in charge of the songs. The film was Berlin's first shot at producing music for a movie. But writing the film's score did not go well for Berlin. The lack of involvement of songwriters in these films often meant songs did not fit into the overall tone of the film. Moreover, Berlin clashed with the George Kaufman, who wrote the dialogue.

Further angering Berlin, the Marx Brothers altered words to his songs without consulting him. Indeed, they would throw in their own routines, ad-libbed lines, and treated songs as "throw-away comic material." Berlin later reflected on his frustration in working both on the stage and the film versions:

> When we started to rehearse we had our plan well formulated. But long suggestions began to come in from the Marx Brothers, from Kaufman, from Harris—in fact, from everybody—and before we knew what had happened the general scheme of things had been turned topsy-turvy. My well laid score was opened up and I wrote new songs, new lyrics, and eventually we had an entirely different production than had been planned.[6]

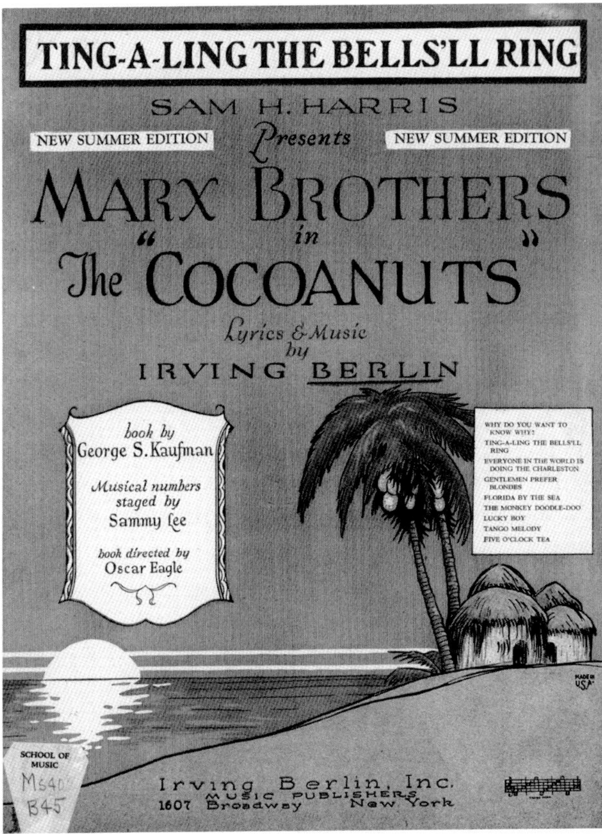

Cover of music sheets for The Cocoanuts *starring the Marx Brothers. One of the early talkies, the film parodies the boom-and-bust of south Florida real estate.* (Courtesy of Irving Gilmore Music Library, Yale University)

Used to being accommodated, Berlin was angry about last-minute songs. He felt the Marx Brothers were parodying his songs, which he strongly objected to. Of course, Berlin had once made a name for himself by parodying other people's songs so his consternation seems misplaced.

He approached the Marx Brothers about leaving his script alone. Groucho Marx, the film's star, had misgiving about the entire project. He quipped about directors Robert Florey and Joseph Santley, "One of them didn't understand English and the other didn't understand comedy."

Berlin was anxious that his songs would fail. Just breaking into film, he knew the stakes were high. He didn't want to be seen as a former Tin

Pan Alley songwriter. After much haggling, the film finally opened. No one seemed too impressed with it, and Berlin's fears about his songs were realized. He composed three songs which fell flat. Film critics pointed out how "far his songs fell from his normally high standards of songwriting."

Berlin learned a lesson about the film industry. Unlike Broadway, the music for films at the time tended to be formulaic love songs. Hollywood often stifled songwriters' creativity. On Broadway, songwriters collaborated closely with producers and directors. But in Hollywood, songwriters were regularly instructed to "just write songs, sometimes without seeing a script."

So Berlin came up with a counter-strategy. He used his considerable influence to insist to studios that he write plot summaries without dialogue to show where his songs could go into the story. This way, his songs would fit into the films. Always the astute businessman, he knew that studios would have to pay him if they had to buy not only his songs but also his script ideas.

Around this time, he developed the story idea for *Mammy*, a film that portrayed the famous singer Al Jolson as part of a touring minstrel show. Minstrel shows portrayed Blacks in a mocking and negative light. They were popular in the late nineteenth century. By the 1930s, they had largely fallen out of favor. *Mammy* was not a minstrel show but rather about the characters who were in a minstrel troupe. Some of the songs allowed for a more intimate expression than stage would allow like "Across the Breakfast Table" and "Let Me Sing and I'm Happy." It was a stretch for Berlin to create songs on this subject and within film's more subtle medium. But Jolson's acting was not as good as his singing. He came across awkwardly in scenes. The film lost a significant amount of money for Warner Brothers. Part of the reason for this financial loss was Jolson's salary. It was larger than the budget for most films.

Soon after, none of the intricacies of the movie business mattered. He would soon encounter a personal tragedy. By late 1928, Irving and Ellin were expecting their second child after their daughter Mary Ellin's birth two years prior. Their son, Irving Berlin Jr., was born on December 1, 1928. He died a few weeks later on Christmas Day. The Berlins were devastated. Christmas had always been Ellin's favorite holiday. It was no longer. Irving felt great sadness. So he did what he always had—like his father—he poured his grief into his music.

Chapter 10

Let's Have Another Cup of Coffee

On October 28, 1929, the Roaring Twenties came to a grinding halt. The stock market crashed. People everywhere lost most of their savings in the market, and many lost their jobs as well. The Hollywood trade magazine *Variety* employed the headline "Wall Street Lays an Egg."

Berlin lost millions of dollars in the collapse of the stock market. Like many investors, he borrowed money to purchase stocks (buying them "on margin"), assuming the stocks would continue going up. This method would allow him to earn multiple times as much money. But he was wrong. When stocks came crashing down, his losses were multiplied.

While Berlin lost millions too, he had something that did not decline—his own song copyrights. That, along with his wife's trust fund, allowed the couple to live relatively unscathed. However, Ellin's extremely wealthy father Clarence Mackay lost almost his entire fortune. In fact, Mackay had the distinction of incurring the largest loss suffered by an individual in the Crash. The Berlins helped him out. Finally, the three, Irving, his wife, and Clarence, were reconciling. It was an irony that Mackay had once looked down on Berlin for being an immigrant songwriter unworthy of his daughter. In the end, it was his songwriting that financially saved Mackay.

As the Depression raged on, the country was devastated. People were losing their jobs, homes, and savings at a pulsating speed. Many were losing hope. President Franklin D. Roosevelt made his famous speech in 1933 assuring that "the only thing we have to fear is fear itself." Many turned to movies and music to escape their troubles.

Broadway continued to be "constricted by the impact of the Depression, cheaper-ticketed movies, and free radio. It was however flourishing musically with satire, politics, and what were called 'smart songs' that combined literate lyrics with beautifully formed melodies over inventive harmonies."[1]

As the country sunk deeper into a depression so did Berlin. For several years, he entered a period of personal despair. "I developed the damnedest feeling of inferiority. There were times between 1930 and 1932 when I got so I called in anybody to listen to my songs—stock room boys, secretaries. One blink of the eye, and I was stuck."[2]

Despite his personal trepidations, or perhaps because of them, Berlin knew how to connect with audiences during the Great Depression. He decided to write topical songs about the depressed economy—but with a positive spin. He composed for a new Broadway musical, *Face the Music.*

The opening scene takes place at an automat, where the formerly affluent who lost almost everything in the Depression, now find their meals. Automats were fast food restaurant where basic foods and drink were served by vending machines. Diners would drop a nickel or a dime in a coin slot and open the door to a box holding a sandwich, dessert, or drink.

The scene is 1932, the low point of the Depression. The chorus describes the formerly rich's new dining environment:

> Come along and you will see
> Mrs. Astor with a grin
> And a dab of ketchup on her chin
> With pearls around her neck
> Mrs. Woolworth waters her mutton,
> And then she splits the check
> With her girlfriend, Mrs. Hutton.

To audiences, Mrs. Astor, Woolworth, and Hutton would be household names as (formerly) extremely rich women.

This scene is followed by the song "Let's Have Another Cup O' Coffee" for a scene where formerly rich patrons eat at a low-cost diner after having lost their fortunes in the stock market crash. The song is upbeat but a bit sarcastic: "Just around the corner, there's a rainbow in the sky. So let's have another cup o' coffee and let's have another piece o' pie."

It was a play on President Herbert Hoover's hollow assertion that "prosperity was just around the corner." He composed other lyrics with similar themes: "Even John D. Rockefeller is looking for the silver lining, Mister Herbert Hoover says that now is the time to buy." History would show that Hoover was right in the long run as the stock market ultimately rebounded handily long after he left office.

Critics praised *Face the Music.* One reviewer, Robert Garland, made a prediction which did not come true. He said the show would still be "running when Mr. Hoover is again and popular and the Empire State Building was filled with tenants." His theatrical critiquing skills were better than his political prognosticating. Hoover was never popular again and was decisively elected out of office in 1932. The Empire State Building did not gain many tenants until well after the show closed.

The show's songs became identified with the Depression. But the most famous Depression-era song was more cutting and written by Yip Harburg and Jay Gorney, "Brother, Can You Spare a Dime?" It struck a chord with listeners around the world and became one of the period's most famous songs.

The Berlins also welcomed another child, Linda, in 1932 and four years later, their third daughter, Elizabeth.

In this period, Berlin composed some of his most famous tunes like "Puttin' on the Ritz," which originally depicted wealthy Black couples in New York's Harlem, and "Heat Wave" for a new Broadway musical, *As Thousands Cheer*. Both songs carried a syncopated rhythm where music and words tugged against each other.

During this time, the theatrical musical was heating up. Audiences were flocking to see stories of love, tragedy, or comedy with musical numbers. Often, actors would dance in them. For musical songwriters, this meant the songs would not be standalones. They would need to advance a story. The songs would need to offer deeper insights into characters. Audiences were used to hearing music in concerts or as part of various skits such as in vaudeville acts or burlesque theater. Now, musicals were becoming more prominent. Audiences would get more used to the idea of suspending their belief. Characters would start singing in a scene and music would accompany them.

This trend was exemplified in the musical *As Thousands Cheer*. Known for not only its music but also its story, it was groundbreaking for its depiction of the extreme racism at the time against Black Americans. Performer Ethel Waters sang the heart-wrenching "Supper Time" about a wife's reaction to the news of her husband's lynching. It reflected the rampant lynchings of Black men that were gripping the South.

The song could have been very preachy. It could have scolded the listener or it could have been overly sentimental. The song worked largely because of its subtlety. By focusing on the woman's concentration on fixing dinner, Berlin created a lyrical marvel of understatement. His song drew upon the character's quiet outrage at the wave of lynchings that spread across the South—and beyond—during the bitter years of the Depression.[3]

Ethel Waters, the actress who sang this song, recalled her experience, noting the contrast between her character and the brutal injustices happening around her versus her well-to-do audiences. She was surprised at their warm reception to the controversial song.

"I was telling my comfortable, well-fed, well-dressed listeners about my people....When I was through and that big, heavy curtain came down, I was called back again and again. I had stopped the show with a type of song never heard before in a revue, and a number that until then had been a question mark."[4]

The cast itself experienced racism too. For the curtain calls, White performers refused to take a bow with the Black actors. As the producer, Berlin responded that there need not be any bows at all. Not wanting to give up their curtain call, the White actors relented. The next night, the White actors took their bows along with the Black actors.

When Berlin was finishing his new musical *As Thousands Cheer*, he hit a stumbling block. He was struggling to close the first act with a strong finish. "I wanted a big Fifth Avenue number. I wanted an old-fashioned type song, but I couldn't come up with anything. The most difficult thing to do is to consciously create an old fashioned tune."[5]

Weeks later, Berlin was still stuck. His songs for the musical were due soon, and he still hadn't stumbled upon the right tune. He experimented with different rhythms and verses. Nothing seemed right. Then, he remembered he had written a few songs that may fit. He rustled through his trunk, which carried old sketches of unpublished songs. He found one from seventeen years prior. He dusted it off and decided to revitalize it for this show. He decided that it had a catchy opening phrase, so he altered the remaining melody and came up with new lyrics for the fashion column number that closed the first act. The song linked fashion to a major holiday, Easter, in keeping with the storyline of the show. What emerged was one of his more popular songs, "Easter Parade." The song depicts the ornately colorful hats and bonnets that adorned women strolling down New York City's glitzy Fifth Avenue in an informal parade in the 1880s when *As Thousands Cheer* took place.

It was a lesson for Berlin. Sometimes the best ideas have already been set forth. He reflected on the song's creation: "A song is like a marriage. It takes a perfect blending of two mates, the music and the words, to make a perfect match. In the case of Easter Parade, it took a divorce and a second marriage to bring about the happiness of unions."

The show was a huge hit, running for 400 performances. That was almost unheard of during the Great Depression. It was also the first Broadway show to give a Black star, Ethel Waters, equal billing with Whites.

As the United States started to recover from the depths of the Depression, the Hollywood musical started to make a comeback as well. Audiences wanted to escape their troubles by watching glitz and glamour on the big screen.

In the early years of talkies, Hollywood's musicals were considered clumsy. Film producers had not figured out how to seamlessly integrate acting with singing in the films with the new sound technology. Composers felt underutilized in working on motion pictures. This included not only Berlin but also the Gershwin brothers, Rodgers and Hart, and others. Film technicians were experimenting with new ways to elegantly film song and dance. Unlike the stage, where exaggerated gestures and big productions soared, film had the potential to allow for close-ups of actors and dancers. Their facial expressions were more important. There was a subtlety and intimacy in the new medium. If only the film producers could figure out how to make all this work.

The Broadway Melody of 1929 is considered the first film musical where these elements came together. The film tells the story of sisters who perform together, portraying their auditions for a *Ziegfeld Follies* type of show and their tribulations on and off stage. It ultimately won the second Academy award for Best Picture. *The Broadway Melody of 1929* spawned other musical "backstage" films. The most notable was *42nd Street* in 1933.

With these successes, Hollywood embarked on a new period of the musical. Struggling deeply with the Great Depression, audiences were more than happy to escape their troubles.

Singer and dancer Fred Astaire was looking for work in film. But his facial features did not show up well on screen tests. The notes from one screen test read, "Can't act. Can't sing. Balding. Can dance a little." Despite these shortcomings, a little-known and formerly bankrupt studio, RKO, took a chance on him. Executives cast him and dancer Ginger Rogers in a new film musical, *Flying Down to Rio*, in 1933. The film was a moderate success but ushered in a wave of new films for the dancing duo of Fred Astaire and Ginger Rogers. One of the most famous was *Top Hat* in 1935.

Berlin was asked to write the score. This time, though, Berlin insisted on a more financially advantageous arrangement. He received a profit-sharing stake and gained more artistic control. Gone were the days when he had to cater to the whims of producers. No longer would he be surprised by how much scripts and his songs had changed without his consent, as he had experienced with *The Cocoanuts.* Now, he would call the shots.

All his songs had to be customized for each character and situation. He was "holed up in his hotel (the Beverly Wilshire Hotel in Beverly Hills, California) for the next six weeks, composing music by night, in his pajamas and slippers, and writing lyrics by day." He created twelve new musical numbers, five of which were used for the film. For the film's featured song "Cheek to Cheek," Astaire had the novel idea to sing the song as though he was talking. Berlin loved the idea. The song

Poster for MGM's Ziegfeld Follies *in Technicolor. It was advertised as the "greatest show of stage or screen."* (Courtesy of Library of Congress, Division of Prints and Photographs)

would become one of the most popular in film history. For decades, it would be sung by countless artists, including Tony Bennett and Lady Gaga, as a duet, in 2014.

Though Astaire liked some of the music, he was displeased with the overall script. Upon reading an early version, he protested. "In the first place—as this book is supposed to be written for me with the intention of giving me the chance to do the things that are most suited to me—I cannot see that my part embraces any of the necessary elements except to dance, dance, dance."[6] Astaire was afraid of being typecast. He also thought his character lacked charm. "He [my character] is an objectionable young man without charm or sympathy or humor."

Producers polled *Top Hat* to select audiences to gauge their reactions. Audiences liked the film but suggested making it slightly shorter and tighter. Around the time the film was to be released though, Berlin received disturbing news from home. His eldest sister Sarah had died at age fifty-three. She fell from the roof of her apartment building. Most, including family members, assumed it was suicide, though that was never confirmed. Sarah had lived a difficult life. Her husband was something of a deadbeat. He was very rough with her and failed to provide an adequate income for their family. She toiled in tough labor conditions. She had never really adjusted to the ways of her newfound country—or learned how it operated—as had her famous younger brother. Berlin did send her a weekly allowance but it was insufficient given her household's low income. A morose Berlin flew back to New York City for his sister's funeral.

He then flew back to Los Angeles for *Top Hat*'s initial run. The film was very successful with critics and at the box office. It ultimately made about three million dollars from ticket sales, turning a handsome profit since it cost just $620,000 (about eleven million in present day dollars) to make it. Maybe even more gratifying to Berlin was that several of the songs he had written made the "Hit Parade." That was a series of the most popular songs played on a Saturday night radio program called *Your Hit Parade.* The program became an important indicator of how the public liked a song based on nationwide surveys, sheet music sales, record sales, band performances, and number of radio plays. "Cheek to Cheek" held the coveted number one spot for weeks. Music publishers and film producers watched the list closely to monitor listener trends.

After *Top Hat,* he wrote the score for another Fred Astaire and

Ginger Rogers film, *Follow the Fleet.* By this point, the dancing duo were famous enough to have films made entirely for them. This film portrayed Fred Astaire as an ex-dancer sailor and Ginger Rogers as a dime-a-dance worker. For Astaire, it was a chance to branch out acting-wise. He had grown tired of always wearing fancy clothes and playing similar roles.

Critics were lukewarm on the film, but audiences liked it a lot. It was a box office success, ending up as the second most profitable show after *Top Hat* among all the Astaire-Rogers series. Berlin's songs in the film, including "I'm Putting All My Eggs in One Basket" and "Let's Face the Music and Dance," made the Hit Parade. He was disappointed, though, that none of his songs in the film received an Oscar nomination.

By 1938, Berlin turned his attention to composing for the new somewhat-autobiographical film *Alexander's Ragtime Band.* He wove a story around many of his most significant songs like "Alexander's Ragtime Band," "Everybody's Doin' It," "Oh! How I Hate to Get Up in the Morning," "A Pretty Girl Is Like a Melody," "Blue Skies,"

Follow the Fleet *movie poster* (Courtesy of the Library of Congress, Division of Photos and Photographs)

"Heat Wave," and "Easter Parade." In this film musical, the history of American popular music told the history of America.

Critics were disappointed in the film. They found it cliché though they lauded some of the musical numbers. The *British Daily Express* opined:

> Every cinematic cliché as it comes up is covered up by the ingredients of the producers, who insist on covering it up with one of Mr. Berlin's more memorable numbers. It is nice not to have to worry about how bored you are with boy-meets-girl, boy-loses-girl. Every time the yawn comes, so does Mr. Berlin to remind you by his melodies of some great point in show business.[7]

Though his songs were popular on the radio, by the late 1930s Berlin was still not fully at ease with the medium. Coming into show business as a Tin Pan Alley songwriter, he still thought of success as the number of sheet music copies sold. He was at first suspicious of radio playing his music for free. By this time, radio was playing a

Irving Berlin and actors from the 1938 film Alexander's Ragtime Band *rehearse songs for the film.* (Courtesy of Wikimedia)

crucial role in more US households, which was direct competition for Berlin. He was critical of the technology, believing that it belittled the value of playing music. He lamented:

> We have become a world of listeners, rather than singers. Our songs don't live anymore. They fail to become part of us. Radio has mechanized them all. In the old days, Al Jolson sang the same song for years until it meant something—when records were played until they cracked. Today, a Hollywood hero sings them once in the films and radio run them ragged for a couple of weeks—then they're dead.[8]

Despite his misgivings, Berlin actually benefited from radio. The medium allowed far many more listeners to hear his songs. In fact, radio multiplied his audiences. Even if a song was not all that popular with audiences or in sheet music sales, it could find success on the radio. For Berlin, this was the song "Say It Isn't So," based on the popular phrase "Say it ain't so, Joe" that a boy had pleaded to famed baseball player Shoeless Joe Jackson about the Black Sox scandal. Berlin also became more open to radio when realizing that a few of his songs from *Top Hat* were also popular plays on the radio.

Chapter 11

God Bless America

The clouds of war were spreading ominously in 1938. The stubborn Depression was lingering, and Americans were in a slump. But movie attendance was up, and 1939 ushered in one of the best years in movies with the *Wizard of Oz, Gone with the Wind, Mr. Smith Goes to Washington,* and other films. Berlin sensed a sharp change in the national mood. With an impending war, he recognized a rise in nationalism. He visited his "trunk" of his old, unpublished songs. He rediscovered his song from 1918, "God Bless America." He based the title on a phrase his mother used to repeat. Despite her poverty and her feeling as an outsider in her new country, Berlin noted that she used to exclaim, "God bless America." That was the basis for the song. During World War I, he was going to use the song for his show *Yip Yip Yaphank*. After trying it in rehearsals, the song seemed over the top. He and others felt it was overly sentimental and sappy.

He noted: "When I saw the show in rehearsals, I realized that the song was just a bit too much. After all, it was a soldiers' show, the boys were in uniform—it was like gilding the lily. I put the piece away and didn't think of it again until that moment in the autumn of 1938."[1]

He put it away and did not think of it until a new war on the horizon. As Americans read daily about the horrors starting to take place in Europe, the national mood in the US had shifted to fear. But Berlin sensed that the national reaction was different this time than from World War I. Accordingly, he adjusted the song to be a "peace" rather than a "wartime" song. So he altered the line, "make her victorious on land and foam" to lyrics that were more tranquil.

From the mountains
to the prairies
to the oceans
white with foam.

Berlin composed the music to build to a climax to emphasize the song's most emotional points. As one biographer noted, "The song builds a melody in wavelike, repeated intervals. Here the sequence of repeated phrases rises to progressively higher notes, then the next phrase begins on the highest note of the song, appropriately enough on the word *God*, which returns, like yet another huge musical wave, to the opening theme of the chorus as the melody, with *home sweet home*, returns to its own home key on the last note."[2]

He then asked famed radio singer Kate Smith to sing the tune. He chose her because he felt she had a powerful voice that would evoke the emotion the song was intended to bring out. Though Berlin was still hesitant about the radio eroding his songs' success as sheet music or record sales, he realized that radio was the better medium for this song. Her radio broadcast was on Armistice Day on November 11, 1938. The song moved something within many listeners. The song crystalized listeners' feelings of patriotism along with a wariness from the Depression and impending war.

The song became an informal national anthem. There were calls for it to replace the "Star Spangled Banner," which had only been the official national anthem since 1931. "God Bless America" was a simple song that anyone could sing. Smith performed it at the 1939 New York World's Fair. The *New York Times* decreed, "Americans who find the *Star Spangled Banner* hard on their voices have found a patriotic song they can sing."[3]

Berlin reflected on the song's success and resonance within much of the population: "The reason *God Bless America* caught on is that it happens to have a universal appeal. Any song that had that is bound to be a success; and let me tell you right here that while song plugging may help a good song, it never put over a poor one…The mob is always right. It seems to be able to sense instinctively what is good, and I believe that there are darned few good songs which have not been whistled or sung by the crowd."[4]

Berlin's personal story as an immigrant who fled pogroms in Russia with his family to find safe harbor in the US gave the song personal meaning. It resonated with the public appeal for tolerance of various groups in stark opposition to the Nazis coming to power in Germany and starting to take over much of Europe.

The *New York Times* referenced the song on November 29, 1938, in covering a performance of the song at a dinner sponsored by the

Kate Smith standing by a radio. She would make "God Bless America" a song recognized in many US households. (Courtesy Library of Congress, Division of Prints and Photographs)

National Conference of Christians and Jews, where religious leaders spoke out against the "doctrine of race and hate" in totalitarian Europe. The speakers warned Americans not to let the same thing happen in their communities. The song was fitting for the occasion.

First Lady Eleanor Roosevelt had the song played in events where she also spoke out against what she saw as the greatest threat to the US at the time: "Fear arising from intolerance and injustice constitutes the chief danger to the country."

But not everyone praised the song. Some patriots shouted down efforts to sing "God Bless America" at public gatherings. Some religious leaders denounced the song as a "specious substitute for religion and patriotism."[5] "America First" patriots rallied around the "Star Spangled Banner" and shuttered at the thought of it being replaced by "God Bless America." Berlin had never proposed that. Some also thought the song was a commercial venture, a product of Tin Pan Alley, and therefore inauthentic as a patriotic song. One editorial writer referred to Berlin as "Izzy Balinsky, ex-Singing Waiter." The article was suggesting that Berlin's ethnic heritage was not appropriately American enough. It's unclear why the writer used "Balinsky," as Berlin's birth last name was Baline.

Some of the backlash showed deep conservative resentment towards immigrants, whom they believed were negatively impacting American culture. When the song was performed at rallies, some booed it. At a joint rally of the Ku Klux Klan and pro-Nazi German American Bund, leaders advocated for boycotting the song.

Berlin was taken aback by the outcry over his song that he believed had a universal appeal. To his further surprise, the song also received substantial pushback from liberals who believed the song was overly jingoistic. They felt the song put America on a pedestal and made it sound like it was better than other countries. Some also said the song has a subtle message of conformity as if to say, "Don't challenge the status quo."

A folk musician from Oklahoma, Woody Guthrie, who would emerge as one of the most important voices of his generation, wrote the song "This Land Is Your Land" largely as a reaction to "God Bless America" being overplayed on the radio. He felt the song had become too commercial and trite. In contrast, his song "This Land Is Your Land" depicted a more realistic America, including its prevalent "No Trespassing" signs. (Later versions omitted several verses and "sweetened" the song.)

In subsequent decades, the song would take on many different roles in social activism as well as in conservative segregationist rallies.

Despite these controversies, Berlin wrote the song with sincerity.

His daughter Mary Ellin Barrett later wrote: "It *was* the land he loved. It *was* his home sweet home. He, the immigrant who had made good, was saying thank you."

Though once written largely from his own immigrant experience, Berlin's "God Bless America" became an iconic song that was used for many political purposes. In the 1940s during labor strikes, it was sung by striking workers as well as by anti-Communist protestors. Strangely, the song was embraced by both sides of the political aisle. During the 1960s, civil rights activists sang it as a call for unity. So did African-American children at school segregation protests in Mississippi and Louisiana. Protestors at rallies led by Martin Luther King Jr. also sang the tune.

Yet during the traumatic mid-1960s as the fight for civil rights continued, "God Bless America" became more of a song for a White, conservative worldview. The lyrics took on a new meaning. Like famed folksinger Woody Guthrie had predicted in the late 1930s, the song came to represent a warning to anyone challenging the status quo. White segregationists took up the song as a personal anthem. In the 1970s, segregationists used the song to oppose school integration of Blacks and Whites. It was a striking irony in that the song itself was written by a Jewish immigrant who saw it as a call to unity. Another irony was that many right-wing activists protested the song when Berlin first wrote it for they did not think an immigrant songwriter should speak for the country. Yet, a generation later, the far right embraced the song.

But the song returned to its universal roots with terrorist attacks on September 11, 2001. The song symbolized the nation's solidarity in the wake of the destruction of the Twin Towers in New York City and part of the Pentagon. Spectators sang the storied tune at vigils, Broadway theaters, and at major league baseball games. Thereafter, it was sung at immigrant rights rallies.

Within a decade, though, the song's controversy reemerged. At a 2013 Major League Baseball (MLB) All-Star Game, Marc Anthony sang the decades-old tune. Though he is a US citizen born of Puerto Rican ethnicity, many social media users questioned why a "foreigner" would sing this song. It was an eerie throwback to the original resistance to Berlin's song.

Sidestepping these controversies, Berlin knew the song would have an important place in US culture. Therefore, he signed over all its royalties to the Boy Scouts and Girl Scouts of America. He remained in control, however, of how the song would be played. He was protective of it. History would show he'd be right. Through the American Society of Composers, Authors, and Publishers (ASCAP), he was able to limit the number of times radio stations played the song. His aim was to prevent overuse. The song had a special sentiment and, if overplayed, it would lose its meaning. Plus, listeners would tire of it. Swing music was all the rage in the 1930s, but Berlin stipulated that there was to be no swing music-version of it.

Radio stations were displeased with Berlin dictating the terms of how his song could be played. One radio station director demanded that Berlin turn over his song to the public. He argued that Berlin had no right to take personal credit for this achievement. The song's inspiration transcended the songwriter. The director wrote in a letter that ran in several newspapers to Berlin: "You, Mr. Berlin, have no more right to a personal interest in 'God Bless America' than the descendants of Abraham Lincoln have a right to restricting copyright on the Gettysburg Address. That great document passed into the public domain as the words fell from his lips. You should be content with nothing more than the glory of having achieved greatness."[6]

Berlin responded that the director's attitude was hypocritical. In fact, the station, according to Berlin, had "defrauded composers and authors of their royalties for a period of years." Ultimately, the radio stations won in that they played the song as many times as they wanted. As predicted, the constant playing wore out the song.

Chapter 12

White Christmas at the Holiday Inn

Berlin sensed another turn in American taste for music. He noticed a new interest in topics about the countryside rather than the cities. They sought comfort and a "hominess" quality in music given the turbulence of World War II. There was a larger change taking place in music taste. The Tin Pan Alley style of music gave way to regional and rural life. Critics wrote that Tin Pan Alley style of music had "lost its freshness and cutting edge." Also, Broadway musicals turned away from revues and multi-musical acts towards a plot-integrated musical like Rodgers and Hammerstein's 1943 smash hit *Oklahoma!* where the songs advance the narrative and reveal more about the characters.

With this in mind, he composed *Holiday Inn* in 1942, a musical about a performer who leaves behind the glitz of New York City for the upstate farm life to open an inn to perform on holidays. It is in this production that his most popular of all songs, "White Christmas," is first sung by Bing Crosby. It would become the best-selling song of all time. He described how he conceived the song in a moment of inspiration in an all-night session. "Sometimes a song is a natural. We (composers) may start it to order for a specific scene or show, but our subconscious beings go to work, and the song is just there. This is what I call a 'round' song."[1]

The song reflects how Berlin felt when he was writing the lyrics. Away from his family while working on the film in Beverly Hills, California, he thought of previous Christmas holidays with his family. His colleagues reflected nostalgically on their childhood Christmas celebrations white with snow. Their stories inspired the song.

Once finished and pitched to Broadway producers, they had little interest in the musical. But Hollywood producers did. Bing Crosby was a star of the early 1940s, and Paramount Pictures decided to cast him in the lead. He played opposite Fred Astaire, who was looking to remake his image after having split with his dance partner, Ginger Rogers.

Irving Berlin composes new tunes on the piano. He was self-taught but could only play in one key. (Courtesy of the Library of Congress, Division of Photos and Photographs)

Album cover to 1942 musical Holiday Inn, *which first featured the song* "White Christmas." *It starred Bing Crosby and Fred Astaire, who would reunite in the film* Blue Skies. (Courtesy of Wikimedia)

The film's song "Abraham," about Abraham Lincoln and how he ended slavery, initially had a racially insensitive lyric. Berlin modified it. Hollywood was slowly changing the way it portrayed people of color.

The film was well-received but its legacy was the song "White Christmas." Not surprisingly, soldiers stationed in the South Pacific during World War II took to the song. Berlin reflected on this phenomenon. "It became a peace song in wartime, nothing I'd ever intended. It was nostalgic for a lot of boys who weren't home for Christmas. It shows that inspiration can produce anything."

The song "White Christmas" was one of the most successful in music history. It stayed at top of the Hit Parade for ten weeks and made the list almost every December for thirteen years. Sales of recordings and sheet music soared into the millions. Bing Crosby's recording is listed in the *Guinness Book of World Record* as the best-selling single of all time. Sales hovered around 50 million copies globally.

While Berlin was working on the film *Holiday Inn,* World War II was escalating. Soon the US was swept into the war with the bombing of Pearl Harbor on December 7, 1941. The government turned to composers for part of its public relations efforts. Aware of the power of music to sway public opinion, the government approached songwriters to compose songs promoting the war's agenda. As one example, the Treasury Secretary requested a song to encourage the purchase of war bonds. Ira Gershwin, the brother of famed and by then deceased George Gershwin, wrote the colloquially titled "Let's Show 'Em How This Country Goes to Town."

Portrait of musical brother team George and Ira Gershwin. They grew up on New York City's Lower East Side and would become some of the best-known songwriters in the early 20th century. (Courtesy of the Library of Congress, Prints and Photographs Division)

Always seizing on the trend in music, Berlin also composed "Arms for the Love of America" for the Ammunition Department and for the American Red Cross he wrote "Angels of Mercy" and the "President's Birthday Ball" for the March of Dimes. The songs' proceeds benefitted these two organizations.

As a former Tin Pan Alley music writer—and once the singing busboy—Berlin had a knack for understanding the common person's tastes. He knew how to move them with simple melodies, direct titles, and emotionality. While his style was not always suited best for musicals with complex story lines and sophisticated films, it was ideal for reaching—and inspiring action from—the average American.

Throughout his career, Berlin had been primarily a commercial musician. That is, one of his primary motivations in composing songs was their profitability. After all, show business is a business. Yet, there were also times when he sincerely wanted to be of service to his nation. He never forgot that had the US not taken in his family—as immigration laws were lax in the 1890s—his family may well have perished. His call to patriotism surfaced most when the US entered war.

Chapter 13

This Is the Army

As the US entered World War II, Berlin decided to write a sequel to *Yip Yip Yaphank* for a new wartime musical called *This Is the Army.* It would play on Broadway with all ticket sales going to the Army Emergency Relief. Berlin cast around three hundred soldiers as performers and crew members. The makeshift theater troupe prepared at Camp Upton in Long Island, New York, where Berlin had been a soldier a generation prior.

He reflected on the differences of the soldiers with whom he served in World War I versus those with whom he was serving in World War II: "The boys are different from those who served in 1918. They had a different upbringing, and the ideals which were held up to them were different. They have seen many of those ideals shattered. They are more serious and grim. They know what they are up against."[1]

As he rehearsed the troops for their first performance, he reflected further on differences in the soldiers between World War I and World War II. He noticed this war carried less pageantry. The overall sentiment was a great sense of worry. He tried to capture this mood in his songs: "Parades are out, cracks, happy songs, all the stock standard forms of patriotism are out of this war. Because this war is too terrible and everybody knows how long and how hard a fight it's going to be for us. This Army makes the other Army, at least while the other Army was on our sill here, look like college boys larking for a big football game. Nowadays, the fellows go off quietly and we watch them go quietly."[2]

There were other important differences. The company performing *This Is the Army* was integrated with White and Black soldiers. White actors wore blackface makeup for the World War I shows for *Yip Yip Yaphank.* This effect was a common practice where instead of hiring Black actors, theaters used White actors with black makeup. Often, they played to racial stereotypes. Yet, in this show, Berlin insisted that

Black and White actors perform together. Berlin believed that the army was the great leveler in society. This notion was true and untrue. Drafted recruits mixed social classes to a certain extent. However, sometimes educated and affluent men found their way out of the draft. Furthermore, Blacks were often excluded from White brigades. During World War II, many Blacks had their own battalions. One of the most famous was the Tuskegee Airmen, who served as military pilots. Sadly, when these wary Black soldiers returned home after the war, they experienced rampant segregation in many areas.

Berlin knew this, of course. But he was determined to integrate his troupe. In his earlier years, he witnessed how the Great War brought together Jewish, German, Irish, and Italian ethnic groups. Though this integration did not include Blacks nor Asians.

Now, decades later in World War II, Berlin hoped that wartime integration would apply to Blacks and Whites. This ideal was important to Berlin, according to some of the soldiers involved in the show. Consequently, the cast for *This Is the Army* was the sole integrated armed services unit during World War II.

This Is the Army *male cast performs in drag. The show raised about $40,000 per week for army expenses.* (Courtesy of Wikimedia Commons)

The show followed closely *Yip Yip Yaphank*, "opening with a minstrel show that led to a vaudeville segment with acrobats, jugglers, and a magician, interspersed throughout with musical numbers, dances, and impersonations. Songs were sentimental, patriotic, and romantic."[3]

This Is the Army opened on Broadway on July 4, 1942, and played for three months, raising over two million dollars for the Army Emergency Relief Fund. Audiences generally loved the show. The showbiz magazine *Variety* declared:

> This Is the Army is the show business sensation of 1942. Opening night was a gala of the grandest sort, something to celebrate in spite of the grim news coming in from most fronts. Fashionably dressed couples crowded into the lobby of the Broadway, mingling with spar-spangled military brass and their well-dressed wives. The house was sold out, though as always, there were a few seats available free of charge to enlisted men.

Some of the most famous, humorous, and easily relatable lyrics about army life in the show were:

> This Is the Army, Mister Jones
> No private rooms or telephones.
> You had your breakfast in bed before
> But you won't have it there anymore

As was often the case with his songs, Berlin was speaking to the average soldier, "Mister Jones." He describes real-life examples of how the army would change one's day-to-day activities such as having breakfast in bed. He invokes the use of the imperative voice with "No private rooms or telephones" to evoke the rule-based atmosphere of the army camps.

Berlin himself appeared in the show to sing his famed "Oh! How I Hate to Get Up in the Morning!" in his World War I uniform. His singing ability did not match his songwriting ability. Still, for a wartime production with a cast of soldiers, audiences did not expect Broadway-quality singing.

First Lady Eleanor Roosevelt saw the show three times. It traveled the US. However, in specific regions, the show ran into problems because its cast was integrated.

One cast member recounted the conflict: "We always insisted that the Black guys stay with us. We wouldn't play in a segregated theater—and that's that. We were invited to a party on occasion, and a couple of times, they didn't include the Black guys. We said, 'We're sorry, we're not coming. Forget it'."[4]

The war-themed play was made into a film, *This Is the Army*. All earnings from the film benefitted the fund as well. A young and little-known actor, Ronald Reagan, who would become the US president about forty years later, starred in it. Berlin also sang his own song in the film. On the set, he was so nervous about performing before the camera that he forgot his own lyrics. After subsequent takes, a crewmember on the set murmured, "If the fellow who wrote that song could hear this guy sing it, he'd roll over in his grave."

The cast of the film toured the world performing for troops at battle sites and in military hospitals to lift their spirits. Berlin underwent

Irving Berlin and other entertainers perform for troops during World War II for Christmas in 1944 in Papua, New Guinea. (Courtesy of the Library of Congress, Division of Prints and Photographs, New York World Telegram and Sun Collection)

the war adversities along with his company often, performing in very dangerous battleground situations. The company performed *This Is the Army* around the world for more than three years to 2.5 million people. At age fifty-seven, Berlin was noted for his service. President Harry Truman awarded him the Medal of Merit at a stately ceremony. Berlin called the ceremony "the biggest emotional experience of my life. Nothing has ever matched this."[5]

Chapter 14

There's No Business Like Show Business

Musicals were changing. In the late nineteenth and early twentieth centuries, they were primarily a series of revues with elaborate dances and costumes such as *Ziegfeld Follies.* They were like vaudeville shows on a grander scale. The scenes were often unrelated. Other early twentieth century musicals were operettas imported from Europe or minstrel shows that often mocked Blacks. In December 1927, the musical *Show Boat* opened at the Ziegfeld Theater. It offered the first "integrated" musical. The storyline, songs, and dances all fit together seamlessly.

Its influence cannot be overstated. Ziegfeld gambled big time on taking on segregation, wife abuse, alcoholism, and other heavy themes for a relatively conservative audience. Rather than standalone songs, now the score advanced the drama.

Composed by Jerome Kern and Oscar Hammerstein II and based on a best-selling book of the same name, the musical portrays the lives of performers, stagehands, and dock workers on a Mississippi riverboat over four decades. The show explores topics like racial discrimination, faith, and tragedy. The most famous songs are "Ol' Man River" and "Can't Help Lovin' Dat Man." It was produced by Florenz Ziegfeld, perhaps the most influential producer on Broadway at the time. He was known primarily for revues so this was new territory even for him.

Revues made a brief comeback during the Great Depression. During 1943, another groundbreaking show furthered the plot-integration musical. That show was *Oklahoma!* from Richard Rodgers and Oscar Hammerstein II. It told the folksy tale based on Lynn Riggs' 1931 play *Green Grow the Lilacs*. The story takes place in 1906 in farm country near the town of Claremore—part of Indian Territory. The plot centers on a love story between a farm girl and two rival suitors: a cowboy and a farmhand.

Playing on Broadway during the height of World War II, the show was a box office smash and ran for an unprecedented 2,212 performances. The musical built on the innovations of *Show Boat*. It, too, was a musical play where the "songs and dances are fully integrated into a well-made story with serious dramatic goals that are able to evoke genuine emotions other than laughter."[1]

Berlin watches an audition with famed composer Richard Rodgers and lyricist Oscar Hammerstein II. Photo is likely from the late 1940s after their smash hit Oklahoma! *that offered songs integrated into the plot.* (Courtesy of the Library of Congress, New York World-Telegram & Sun Collection, Al Aumuller, World Telegram staff photographer)

Amid this backdrop, Berlin knew he had to somewhat change his approach to musicals. After the war ended in 1945, Broadway turned its attention back to entertaining audiences during peacetime. A weary American public was looking to put the war behind them. Broadway writers were looking for fresh material.

As a playwright and composer, Dorothy Fields personified this new style of the plot-integrated musical. She would say that she was a "book writer," meaning script writer, even when she was working on songs. She also noted that she never tried to write the next hit song. Rather, she was writing a song to fit into a spot in the show. It was like molding a piece to fit into the puzzle.

She thought of a novel idea for a musical inspired by a story a friend told her about a young soldier visiting an amusement park at Coney Island. "He had kewpie dolls and lamps and every piece of junk you could possibly win. How come? Across his chest, he had a row of sharp-shooter medals. And as if out of the sky, from Heaven, comes this idea... Annie Oakley, the sharpshooter!"[2] Annie Oakley was a performer in Buffalo Bill's traveling Wild West show. A musical about her seemed like a novel idea.

Broadway producers agreed, and the show was a go. Dorothy was to work with her brother, Jerome Kern, on the book and music. But tragedy soon struck. Jerome had a stroke and died suddenly.

Looking to save their show, they approached Berlin to write the score. But he hesitated. He was unsure about writing music with a rustic theme—what he dubbed "hillbilly music." Berlin was used to jagged show tunes with an urban beat. But he realized that *Annie Get Your Gun* was ultimately a musical about show business, not country people, and his show tune style of composing would work. He also related to the main character Annie Oakley, a "poor, uneducated, feisty, and enormously talented performer."[3] Berlin, too, had come from an impoverished background though he grew up mostly on the streets of New York's Lower East Side versus the rugged Ohio countryside from which Annie came.

Berlin struggled to give his show songs the right dialect. He then remembered the advice another songwriter gave him. "You can achieve folksiness by dropping the final letters from words." He writes one of the show's key songs: "Doin' What Comes Natur'lly."

Yet with an eye to show business, he wrote the show-stopping tune, "There's No Business Like Show Business." Berlin liked to try his songs out on his friends, colleagues, or "anyone who would listen" to elicit their reactions. He sang it for his secretary, who dismissed it. If one looked bored or distracted as he sang it, he was apt to shelve or modify the song. He sang it for Rodgers and Hammerstein and others, who were too stunned to give their reaction. Berlin took their hesitation as a rejection and tossed aside the song.

Later, he realized that he misread their reactions. They loved the song. He raced to his office with his secretary and frantically looked for the music sheet he had thrown away. The song that was destined to become one of the musical theater's most popular songs was almost lost until later discovered under a phone book. When *Annie Get Your Gun* opened in 1946, it ended up producing more hit songs from the cast album than any show before or since.

In a way, *Annie Get Your Gun* was a mixture of the old Tin Pan Alley style tunes that Berlin had built his career on as well as the new integrated musical where the songs advanced the plot or portrayed characters more deeply. With the show's success, Berlin found a confidence in composing music and lyrics for this new type of show.

Audiences liked the show more than critics. Some dismissed it as cliché or "insufficiently innovative." But all agreed that Berlin's score was outstanding and made the musical memorable. Berlin reveled in the success and was perhaps a bit defensive of it. One friend remarked that *Annie Get Your Gun* was old fashioned. "Yeah," Berlin retorted, "a good old-fashioned smash."

Puttin On the Ritz

He then capitalized on this success for the 1946 film *Blue Skies* with Bing Crosby and Fred Astaire, who was no longer appearing much with his former dance partner, Ginger Rogers. The storyline was mediocre. Most memorable from the film was Berlin's dance number "Puttin' on the Ritz" with its catchy tune. To "put on the ritz" meant to dress very fashionably. The opulent Ritz Hotel inspired the term. Berlin had composed the song in 1927. It was featured in the musical film *Puttin' on the Ritz* in 1930. Back then, the song had a different—and somewhat racially condescending—meaning. The song portrayed well-dressed but impoverished Blacks in New York City's Harlem strutting up and down Lenox Avenue. In his new version, the theme

Famed theater actress Ethel Merman and Ray Middleton star in the musical Annie Get Your Gun, *depicting sharpshooter Annie Oakley.* (Courtesy of Wikimedia)

A lobby card displaying a scene from the film Puttin' on the Ritz *starring Joan Bennett and James Gleason.* (Courtesy of Wikimedia)

changed, illustrating the changes in racial attitudes and acceptability in the intervening two decades. Now, the song centered on the "well-to-do" Whites parading up and down Park Avenue. That avenue was known for its wealthy residents who often lived in a "bubble," as they were unaware or indifferent to less prosperous areas of the city. Music critics note that the rhythmic pattern is among the most provocative they had heard.

When Fred Astaire was making the film, he had a major announcement. *Blue Skies* would be his last film with dancing on camera. *Puttin' on the Ritz* was to be his final dance performance on film. (After the making of the film, Astaire still acted in movies, television, and theater and continued to perform more modest dance numbers.) He wanted to go out with a bang. So he put in "five weeks of back-breaking physical work" on the number, filming the complex number eight times to create seven images of himself dancing as his own mirror-like chorus. After the final take, he supposedly threw off his toupee and proclaimed, "Never, never. Never will I have to wear this blasted rug again!"[4]

Album cover for the soundtrack to the 1946 film Blue Skies *with Bing Crosby and Fred Astaire, both huge stars at the time. The film has been largely forgotten over time.* (Courtesy of Wikimedia Commons)

Judy Garland in Easter Parade

By 1948, Berlin was working on the film for *Easter Parade,* to star Judy Garland. Like previous films, Berlin had already written the title song so his task was to write the remainder of the score. In negotiating his contract terms, Berlin drove a hard bargain. He insisted on a percentage of the film's profits as well as a hefty salary. Louis Mayer, a head of MGM Studios, reluctantly agreed. He knew that Berlin was famous enough to have the better hand in negotiating. Berlin refused the flat fee of $500,000. Eventually, Berlin held out for $600,000 plus a percentage of the film's profits.

Judy Garland starred in the picture, and her husband Vincente Minnelli was to direct the film. One day, the producers called in Minnelli—to fire him. A stunned Minnelli asked why. They explained that his wife had asked for his removal. Given her ailments and high stress levels, she felt it too burndensome to both live and work with her director. The producers complied with her wishes. Minnelli was replaced by an unknown director.

The show was light and depicted New York's vaudeville and *Ziegfeld Follies* during 1912. The film was somewhat of a vehicle—or a movie made to showcase famous actors—for Judy Garland and Gene Kelly. But Kelly broke his ankle playing volleyball prior to produciton. So Fred Astaire replaced him. His retirement from film was short-lived. *Puttin' on the Ritz* was to have been his last film musical sequence. But fate intervened. *Easter Parade* actually revitalized Astaire's career.

Despite the chaos behind the scenes, the film was was one of the highest-grossing musical films at the box office in 1948. Berlin's

Easter Parade *movie poster from 1948.* (Courtesy of the Library of Congress, Division of Prints and Photographs)

Photo of Irving Berlin around the time he was making Easter Parade *in the 1940s.* (Courtesy of Wikimedia)

negotiating for a piece of the revenue paid off handsomely. Critics lauded it. One called it "the most joyous of the year." Despite its financial and critical success, the film never really became a classic. Perhaps the most memorable songs in it were "Steppin' Out with My Baby," "We're a Couple of Swells," and "I Love a Piano."

Fresh with this film's success, Berlin then turned to another project: *Miss Liberty*. His idea was to write a musical about the experience of immigrants coming to the US. He wrote a song derived from poet Emma Lazarus's "The New Colossus" inscribed on the Statue of Liberty. The most famous lines from that sonnet were "Give me your tired, your poor, your huddled masses yearning to breathe free." They inspired immigrants primarily from eastern and southern Europe to come to the US in search of a better life.

Her sonnet recast the Statue of Liberty. A gift from France, it was initially a symbol of freedom from tyrany. Lazarus's poem reframed it as a light of hope for disenfranchised individuals everywhere. It was to stand in contrast with the "Old Colussus," which was a huge statue on the island of Rhodes, Greece, around 200 AD. (It was destroyed in an earthquake not long after.) That statue was about keeping foreigners away. Conversely, Lazarus's New Colossus was about inviting them in.

Berlin composed a song from this sonnet called "Give Me Your Tired." His hope was that this song would be as stirring and impactful as "God Bless America." Berlin wrote other songs for the show. But he seemed to return to his Tin Pan Alley roots in writing a series of one-off numbers to become hits. He did not put his focus on composing a plot-integrated musical to reveal wishes and thoughts of the characters. Critics unfortunatley took notice.

Brooke Atkinson in the *New York Times* called it a "disappointing musical comedy . . . done to a worn formula . . . put together without sparkle or originality." Other critics lamented that Berlin missed a key opportunity to write a musical about a subject as personal to the US as the Statue of Liberty.

One blunt critic, Hobe Morrison, bemoaned that the show "had the faults of an over-plotted book, undistinguished score, insufficient comedy and merely adequate performances." Not only did the show fare poorly with critics and at the box office but none of the individual songs were hits. That was the standard Berlin used to measure his success earlier in his career.

In a July 18, 1949, letter to composer Kurt Weill, Berlin acknowledged the poor critical reception but thought the play would resonate with audiences. "As you know, we got very bad notices from the important papers, but I feel this is an audience show, and we can overcome the bad reviews. In any event, I hope so."[5]

Berlin's hope for a box office success was not realized.

A Show about Politics—Call Me Madam

Berlin learned that not all shows could be hits. His next venuture in 1950 was about a prominent socialite widow in Washington DC. In return for her sizable campaign contributions to President Harry Truman, he appointed her ambassador to a small fictionalized European country. It was based on Perle Mesta. A theater producer spotted an article in the newspaper. He called Berlin and said he had a great idea for a show. That show would become *Call Me Madam*, a satire on American on politics.

Ingrid Vardund stars as Sally Adams in a Norwegian version of Call Me Madam. (Courtesy of the National Archives of Norway, Wikimedia)

The show portrayed the unlikely ambassador's arrival to the fictional European country. She knew nothing about the country. One of the opening songs, "Hostess with the Mostess'," was a catchy number about Sally Adams, the fictional character who mirrored Perle Mesta, who was known for her vibrant parties back in Washington DC. The plot centers on her romantic relationship with a local politician. Through a series of innocent mishaps, she meddles in the local election. That, of course, is a flagrant violation of the ambassadorship and President Harry S. Truman recalls her.

After his failure with *Miss Liberty*, Berlin was determined to make this show a success. Berlin commented in interviews that he had worked harder and more urgently on the show than probably any other. *Miss Liberty* had failed to recoup its investment and left many involved feeling bruised. Ethel Merman meanwhile had grown tired of starring in musicals and preferred to be in a drama. Since *Call Me Madam* was based on a real person, Berlin and his team had to tread lightly to ensure they would not receive liability lawsuits for grossly misportraying Ms. Mesa.

As opening night drew nearer, producers grew confident in the show. They decided to charge $7.20 for orchestra seats, which was a Broadway record. They gambled that by upping the price, theater goers would still purchase tickets. This way, they would recoup their profit faster.

The show opened with a record advance sale of two million dollars. The producers' bet of raising orchestra seat prices had paid off. Critics were mixed on the show. The *Boston Record* noted that the show had "only an occasional flash of inspirational fire." Berlin credited Ethel Merman's stellar performance for the success of the show: "Give her [Ethel Merman] a song, and she'll make it sound good. Give her a good song, and she'll make it sound great. And you'd better write her a good lyric, because when she sings the words, the guy in the last row of the balcony can hear every syllable."[6]

Perhaps one of the most overlooked parts of the score was Irving Berlin's prescience that General Dwight Eisenhower would become the eventual president in 1952. At the time the show was written, both the Republicans and Democrats were courting the esteemed general. Very few thought he would win the election, which was still a few years away.

For the first—and maybe only—time, a Broadway song became a presidential campaign slogan. This song was "They Like Ike," referring to General Dwight D. Eisenhower, a presidential hopeful. A few years later when Eisenhower did indeed run for office, the slogan was adapted to "I Like Ike." At a campaign rally for Eisenhower at Madison Square Garden, Berlin sang "I Like Ike." It would become one of the most successful campaign slogans in political history.

In 1954, he set out to make the film *White Christmas*. The title came from his song of the same title first performed in his film *Holiday Inn* twelve years earlier. It was the best-selling Christmas song of all time. He had originally conceived of it as a stage musical but it ended up as a film. It was to star Fred Astaire and Bing Crosby just as *Holiday Inn* had.

But chaos reigned during the film's production. Bing Crosby got cold feet. Fred Astaire was lukewarm on the story and after reading the script left the show. He had been disappointed by scripts since *Top Hat* and was impatient with stock characters and formulaic storylines. The cast and crew started to worry that the film was doomed. Discouraged, Berlin forged ahead with composing nine new songs for the struggling film. *White Christmas* has a heavy sentimental quality. It seemed to some overwrought, predictable, and flat.

In some ways, it was technology that saved the film. It was the first movie to be made in VistaVision, a widescreen process developed by Paramount Pictures that allowed widescreen cinematography and a higher resolution. It gave film a more realistic look. The memorable songs from the film were recycled from Berlin's earlier works, including "White Christmas," "Heat Wave," and "Blue Skies."

Despite the film's production troubles, *White Christmas* soared at the box office. The film was one of the top moneymakers in 1954. Critics, though, were mixed. *The New York Times* praised the fine pictorial quality resulting from the use of VistaVision but lamented, "It is too bad that it doesn't hit the eardrums and the funny bone with equal force." Other critics were more favorable towards the film.

Chapter 15

Out of Tune

From this film, Berlin went on to produce *There's No Business Like Show Business*. But Berlin's mood had begun to sour. He was suffering from depression. "I got really sick, I worried about everything, when, really, I had nothing to worry about." Though Berlin was an internationally famous songwriter, he still experienced stage fright at times. It was reported that when Berlin invited Bing Crosby to his house to hear the score for *White Christmas*, Berlin was overcome with fear. In some ways, he regressed back to his youthful days when he would have to perform in front of important Broadway producers. Crosby then thoughtfully asked if Berlin liked the songs he had composed for the film. When Berlin said he did, Crosby said "they are good enough for me."

Perhaps Berlin's fear in performing his songs for Crosby was an onset of his self-doubt. This feeling was not new for Berlin. There were many times he felt insecure as a composer. But by the late 1950s, it seemed different. Lots of plans for Berlin to compose scores for musicals and films in this period did not materialize. Others he turned down. Most significantly, the estate of George Bernard Shaw offered the play *Pygmalion* for Berlin to convert into a musical. But Berlin turned it down. The musical that ensued was *My Fair Lady*, one of the most successful in Broadway history. A musical he was going to compose about postwar Japan also never came to be.

By 1959, depression had set in for the aging composer. He later wrote: "There was everything a man could want. Money? It no longer meant anything. It came in, went out. It would always come in, I decided to quit, to retire. I took up painting. Painting? That's a laugh. Daubs. They were awful. They had no meaning. I wrote no music, I made no songs, I idled. For five years, first health troubles. Nerves, ague pains, twitches. Then depression. I got to a point I didn't want to leave my room when daylight came."[1]

As Berlin was wrestling with insomnia and depression, the music world around him was changing. That had always been the case, of course. When he first began as a youth, "pluggers" and "buskers" would sing tunes at restaurants, cafés, and at other venues. Tin Pan Alley ruled the music business with its publication, promotion, and sales of music sheets. The only way households could hear music was at a concert or by purchasing sheet music and playing the tune at home. Recorded music and phonographs changed music. But probably nothing did like the radio.

During Berlin's time not only did the distribution of music change but also its style. Around 1910, Berlin was hailed as the ragtime king. A decade later, though, the nation's music taste had turned to jazz, blues, and big band music. Musicals were largely grown out of vaudeville with a collection of one-off skits, songs, and comedy routines. In 1927, *Show Boat* was the first "integrative musical" where songs advanced the plot and showcased characters.

Throughout all these changes and more, Berlin adjusted. He always had an ear to what the audience or listener liked. Berlin seemed to have his finger on the pulse of the American—and international—buyer.

Rock and Roll

By the late 1950s, the musical landscape changed again. This time, though, Berlin seemed unable to adjust. Time was beginning to leave Berlin behind. He still composed popular tunes and shows, but the failures outnumbered the successes. He lamented, "Who is going to tell me that I'm washed up as a songwriter? That day is sure to come, and I'm always afraid my friends won't have the courage to tell me. I don't want to make my exit in the midst of a bunch of mediocre songs. I want my last one to have just as much merit as my first."[2]

Worse yet, Berlin began to lose his confidence once more. He always had an "ear" for what the public craved. The public loved Elvis Presley and rock and roll, and Berlin seemed out of tune. Americans were getting their first color televisions and listening less to the radio. Berlin once commented, "A song is like a marriage. It takes a perfect blending of the two mates, the music, and the words, to make a perfect match."[3] But now it seemed that the "match" was no longer in step with the times.

Perhaps the biggest musical shift in this era was the song "Rock

Around the Clock." The tune was among the first rock and roll songs. The recording by Bill Haley & His Comets in 1954 for American Decca became a number one single in both the US and in Europe. Haley's recording became an anthem for rebellious 1950s youth and is widely considered to be the song that brought rock and roll into mainstream culture around the world.

Showcasing its significance, Bill Haley & His Comets performed the song on one of the most highly rated shows on nascent television: *Texaco Star Theater* hosted by Milton Berle. Months later, the band performed on the famed *Ed Sullivan Show*'s Toast of the Town. With television in many US households by the mid-1950s, performing on music shows was key for success. It was something that Berlin never grew accustomed to. In 1957, Haley toured Europe bringing rock and roll to that continent.

Bill Haley & His Comets along with other acts perform to eager audiences in Europe. They would usher in rock and roll as a dominant rock genre. (Courtesy of Wikimedia)

"Rock Around the Clock" ushered in a new era of rock and roll. Jim Dawson's book, *Rock Around the Clock: The Record that Started the Rock Revolution,* shows how the song eclipsed the music industry and listener taste around the globe. Indeed, the song is cited as the "biggest-selling vinyl rock and roll single of all time." At least twenty-five million copies were sold. It's considered the second biggest selling song of all time. The first, ironically, was Irving Berlin's 1942 "White Christmas" sung by Bing Crosby. (*The Guinness Book of World Records* discontinued the category in the 1970s.)

Haley re-recorded the song but later versions never caught on as much as did the original. The original version was used in the iconic and groundbreaking film about teenagers, *American Graffiti,* and later on the hit TV series *Happy Days* for its first two seasons.

Elvis Presley also took the music scene by storm. Hailing from Tupelo, Mississippi, Presley was hailed the "King of Rock and Roll" or by some as the "King." The title of "King" had once been bestowed on Berlin as the king of ragtime. But now it was Presley who was the upstart. He was considered a pioneer of "rockabilly, an up-tempo, backbeat-driven fashion of country music and rhythm and blues." His first smash hit "Heartbreak Hotel" in 1956 catapulted him to the heart of the music scene. "With a series of successful network television appearances and chart-topping records, he became the leading figure of the newly popular sound of rock and roll. His energized interpretations of songs and sexually provocative performance style, combined with a singularly potent mix of influences across color lines during a transformative era in race relations, made him enormously popular—and controversial."[4]

Amid this new world of rock and roll, Berlin seemed lost. He was never fully comfortable with the radio and how it played songs for "free." Though he grew accustomed to it, he never truly understood how to leverage this technology, much less that of television. Always on the air, radio shows constantly needed content. Therefore, they played songs over and over. Often, they "wore them out" as listeners grew tired of the songs. As a result, a song's shelf life decreased.

Consequently, Berlin felt, as did many composers, that the quality of songwriting decreased.

A music producer summarized the industry's sentiment by the late 1950s:

> No Artist & Repertory (A&R) man [music producer] is going to turn down a song he thinks is a hit. We need hits to keep our jobs. If a songwriter like Irving Berlin were to write a new song tomorrow, the chances are that any producer would jump to record it, but I'm not going to keep recording Berlin's old hits, just because they're Berlin's. What some of the old-timers don't realize is that Tin Pan Alley isn't the heart of the music world anymore. Hits today can spring up from any part of the country and on any one of some 700 record labels.[5]

A closer look at the music industry reveals that the songs that played on the radio were not as a result of the free market. In fact, record companies bribed radio disc jockey to play their songs. Of course, the music industry had always been compromised. Decades prior, Tin Pan Alley publishers bribed stars to promote their stars by printing their names on sheet music and giving them a share of the profits.

Berlin had to face another reality. Songwriters were becoming less important. Singers would often re-interpret a song. There was nothing new about artists taking on different meanings to a song but the trend became more pronounced during the late 1950s rock and roll period. Moreover, performers began to increasingly write the lyrics and music to their own songs. Consequently, the role of lyricist or composer declined. Broadway musicals became less about producing hit songs and known more for the musicals themselves. Casts began producing albums showcasing all the songs in one LP (long playing album). Also, in certain cases, musical numbers in shows became secondary to the storyline.

Berlin felt lost amid these developments. But by the early 1960s, he briefly felt reinvigorated. He was ready to return to songwriting. Throughout Berlin's life, songwriting had been his solace after the sudden death of his first wife, the loss of his son, or as a struggling singing waiter in his youth. Berlin recounted his return to songwriting: "One day, after five years of it, I looked at myself and said, 'What you need is to go back to work. What made you think you could ever quit?' It was wonderful. I threw out the medicines, paid off the doctors, and sat down and did what for almost sixty years I have done best—I started writing music again. My spirits soared, my aches and pains disappeared."

He then offered advice: "I want every man with any kind of talent to look at me and heed—don't quit. Don't turn your back on the mystery of talent, don't abandon what was given to you, don't scorn your gifts. Use them until your last day on earth and live a full, rich, and rewarding life."

His thoughts were powerful. Sadly, though, in future years, he did not heed his own advice. He was ready to write a new musical. He approached his collaborators Howard Lindsay and Russel Crouse from *Call Me Madam*, which foreshadows the win in real life of General Dwight Eisenhower.

Mr. President

Continuing with this political theme, Lindsay and Crouse presented the idea of a musical about a president after he leaves office. It would be a comic spin on the post-presidency of President John F. Kennedy. As this was the early 1960s and Kennedy was still in office, no one knew what that would look like, which made the musical more creative. Tragically, what no one could have known then was that Kennedy would be assassinated in November 1963. Sadly, he would never have a post-presidency.

So in early 1962, Berlin was back writing songs for a musical. It was a familiar yet distant feeling. He wanted to prove to others, the press, and especially to himself that he could still compose fresh songs. He remembered that he had old songs in his trunk he could dig out. But he didn't want to rely on those. He wanted to create something new—as he had in the past. Never entirely comfortable with the integrated musical, he composed songs to advance the story.

But he still tried to conceive hit songs—even if they did not fit squarely into the story. He confided to a reporter, "I tried to write a little closer to the book [the script], but I hate that term integrated score. If you have a great song, you can always integrate it into any show."[6]

The show, *Mr. President*, opened to disastrous reviews. The theater critics did not pull any punches. One compared it to the voyage of the *Titanic*. Another compared the prosaic lyrics to "mere wooden soldiers keeping up with the beat." The show also bombed at the box office.

The question of musical integration—whereby the songs advance the plot and/or showcase more about characters—resurfaced in interviews. A Tin Pan Alley songwriter at heart, Berlin was never totally comfortable with the subject. He didn't agree with how "integrative musicals" were conceptualized.

He later told a friend, "We tried to integrate the score. Everybody integrates. All the ballads are woven into the score. I tried to make them a part of the script—general songs that fit the situation."

He further noted that he did "not want the songs to be so firmly threaded into the plot that they could not be sung, and enjoyed, outside the theater." And he hoped they would be popular. "Certainly, I want hits. Hits represent that the song is good."[7]

His songs for *Mr. President* integrated into the storyline but perhaps not enough for critics or audience members. Many called out the score for being "corny" and over-the-top patriotic. Berlin was disappointed with the show's lackluster sales. But, in some ways, he was happy to be back in the music world—even if critics and audiences were unpleased with his latest work. It was a long five-year hiatus. Berlin wanted to be back.

Critics were unkind to the show. But Berlin had hoped it would still be a box office hit. It was not. His letter to his colleague, composer and lyricist Harold Rome, reveals his feeling at the time of the opening: "Thanks for that very nice wire for the opening. As you know, we weren't liked by the critics, but we do have a so-called 'audience' show, which isn't too bad."[8]

With a surprising amount of excitement, Berlin approached Arthur Freed at MGM with whom he had worked prior. Berlin proposed a movie with some of his greatest hits as well as some new tunes. Freed envisioned the film as a biography of Berlin featuring his songs with dance and a lavish production. After all, a film needs a story. It cannot be simply a collection of songs.

But Berlin was wary of biographies. He was mortified by *Yankee Doodle Dandy*, a film about his mentor George Cohan. Though the film was critically acclaimed, Berlin felt it was syrupy and overly sentimental, which ironically were what many judged some of his songs and plays as. He was even less impressed by films about other composers. He shuddered at the thought of a biography on himself. He also relished his privacy. He did not want his story told in a public format during his lifetime. He insisted on the film featuring a collection of his songs.

Yet, a series of songs does not a film make. Freed explained his concerns: "In the old days, all you needed was the money to develop the negative and the picture would make a profit. You didn't need a book. You just strung the songs together, threw in a few dance routines and that was a musical. Now you need a script. It's more important than stars. You need choreography. It's tough enough to make a buck with an ordinary movie. And it's even tougher with a musical."[9]

Freed pushed hard for the film and began its initial casting. Yet, the film's demise came from management changes at MGM. The new leadership cancelled the film.

Berlin also collaborated with Goddard Lieberson of CBS Records on making an album of his key songs throughout the decades. His February 8, 1968, letter to Lieberson shows his perspective on how the compilation should be done.

"I tried to unscramble the many ways of doing the album and I feel pretty sure that your idea of doing it chronologically, along with the pictures, is the right way. That is, starting from the immigrant angle, coming to America from Russia, using a few of the pictures you have of the period, including those of my father, mother, and those of me as a boy. Then, as a biographical piece of the Lower East Side including a picture of Cherry Street, where I lived."[10]

One Last Hit Show

But then Berlin's luck turned around. Sometimes, his biggest hits were waiting in his trunk or in shows from decades prior that were ripe for a revival. In 1966, Richard Rodgers decided to stage a renewal of *Annie Get Your Gun* at New York City's Lincoln Center. The center had just opened a few years before in what was a run-down part of Manhattan. The building of Lincoln Center was part of the city's urban renewal effort. The idea was to attract visitors and tourists to less desirable neighborhoods. The plan would be a huge success. The neighborhood would one day become one of the most affluent and culturally rich in the world.

The revival was to star once again Ethel Merman. Though she was older, everyone felt she could still play the part of Annie Oakley well. Berlin updated the score, adding a new number or two and refreshing some of the melodies. With a nod to the women's liberation movement, Berlin altered some lyrics accordingly. The revival was a big success. Critics praised it, and audiences bought tickets. It was the comeback that Berlin had dreamed of for years. He was seventy-eight years old and had a hit on his hands.

In some ways, the revival was his goodbye to the public. Though he had managed to squeak out another hit, the world around him continued to change. Berlin felt more alienated. His failures haunted him. He lamented, "At my age, it's hard to go to auditions and rehearsals and the rest. Besides, you get frightened. You can stand success, but you're afraid of failure."

Ed Sullivan delivered a tribute of Berlin's music in the late 1960s. Berlin's letter to popular lyricist and librettist Yip Harburg shows his ill ease about his image. Berlin wrote in a letter to Harburg dated May 10, 1968: "The reaction to the Sullivan tribute is great and, of course, I'm delighted. I wasn't too concerned about the show because Sullivan has a built-in audience and is always good, but I was worried about my personal appearance. However, everyone seems to think it was OK."[11]

By the late 1960s, he had closed the door of the house near the United Nations he had been living in for forty years. He and his wife essentially went into a self-imposed reclusiveness. They rarely left home. He once said, "There's a whole new public out there, and they don't even know people like me are still around. We're antiques, museum pieces. Today, it's all kids."

Music had totally changed—as it always had. But Berlin, now in his eighties, was out of step. He very seldom ventured out to attend parties or gatherings. He was also very protective about granting rights for his music. Always the businessman, he wanted to ensure the right amount of royalties were paid. But it was more than that. He wanted to make sure that his songs were performed in the right spirit.

In his late eighties and nineties, not surprisingly, he struggled with his health. His entire life he had struggled with insomnia. Working as a singing waiter in his youth, he stayed up all night. He never seemed to shake that schedule.

There were exceptions to his reclusiveness. Most notably in 1973, he attended the White House for a concert to perform "God Bless America" with President Richard Nixon. The multi-act event was bittersweet though. Richard Nixon and his White House compatriots were caught up in the beginning of the Watergate scandal that would ultimately bring down his presidency.

During his retirement years, Berlin enforced his copyrights of music. *Mad* magazine, a humor publication, printed a farcical version of "A Pretty Girl Is Like a Melody." Berlin and his attorneys were not amused. They sued the magazine for copyright infringement. A judge, however, ruled that the parody had merely borrowed from the original. His final judgment was that the magazine had not violated Berlin's copyright protections. An appellate judge upheld the decision. The case against *Mad* was concluded in favor of the magazine.

The public never forgot Berlin's songs nor his personage. In late December, for many years, Christmas carolers would gather outside his home hoping to catch a glimpse of the once-famous songwriter. But they never did. One year, a worker at the house came out to offer the carolers hot chocolate and told them that Mr. Berlin thanked them.

In 1987, the great dancer Fred Astaire passed away. A year later, Berlin's wife died. In 1988, at Carnegie Hall entertainers presented a night of his songs as a one-hundred-year tribute to the prolific composer. Yet, Berlin declined to attend or to watch it remotely.

Heartbroken from the death of his wife and secluded from the world, in September 1989, at the age of 101, Berlin died in his apartment.

Irving Berlin and his family's residence on Beekman Place on Manhattan's East Side. Berlin lived in the neo-Georgian brick town houses built in the 1930s from 1946 until his death in 1989. (Courtesy Wikimedia Commons)

A sign commemorates Berlin's residence in the Beekman Place residence. (Courtesy of Wikimedia Commons)

Berlin is America's most prolific songwriter. His songs are still played around the world, though many listeners probably don't know he was the songwriter. "Berlin's melodies were something Americans had in common, like the weather, the Depression, the bittersweet memories of romance or a vanished youth."[12] Berlin always said he sought to capture the heart of the average American.

With generations of listeners singing his tunes like "White Christmas" during the Christmas season or "God Bless America" during times of national strife like during September 11, 2001, as well as many seventh inning stretches during baseball games, he has surely done so. In 2018 and 2019, his plays *Holiday Inn* and *Call Me Madam* were revived on Broadway and Off-Broadway respectively. His hit songs like "Cheek to Cheek" are performed by modern superstars like Lady Gaga in duet with Tony Bennett. A musical about his life also played to packed audiences in 2018.

And with that, his music lives on.

Notes

Chapter 1

1. Edward Jablonski, *American Troubadour* (New York: Henry Holt, 1999), 3.
2. Mary Antin, *From Plotzk to Boston: A Young Girl's Journey from Russia to the Promised Land* (New York: Markus Wiener, 2003).
3. Jablonski, *American Troubadour,* 8; original source unknown.
4. Irving Berlin: The Voice of the City (BBC Bristol and A&E Network), 1988.
5. Jablonski, 13.
6. Tom Streissguth, *Say It with Music: A Story about Irving Berlin* (Minneapolis: Carolrhoda Books, 1994), 10.

Chapter 2

1. Streissguth, *Say It with Music,* 13.
2. Philip Furia, *Irving Berlin: A Life in Song* (New York: Schirmer Books, 1998), 12.
3. Ibid.

Chapter 3

1. "Vaudeville," Ultimate Pop Culture Wiki, last modified December 2019, ultimatepopculture.fandom.com/wiki/vaudeville.

Chapter 4

1. Streissguth, *Say It with Music,* 25.
2. Ibid.
3. Benjamin Sears (voice) and Bradford Connor (piano), liner notes, *Keep on Smiling: Songs by Irving Berlin, 1915-1918* (Oakton Recordings, 1996), CD.
4. Streissguth, *Say It with Music,* 30.

Chapter 6

1. Bruce Catton, "He Wanted to Murder the Bugler," American Heritage 18, no. 5 (August 1967).
2. Max Wilk, They're Playing Our Song (New York: Atheneum, 1973), 275.
3. Parts of dialogue taken from Streissguth, *Say It with Music*, 39.
4. Benjamin Sears, "Yip! Yip! Yaphank!," American Classics, americanclassicsmusic.org/yip-yip-yaphank/.

Chapter 7

1. Brooklyn Daily Eagle, April 24, 1921, 12.
2. Jablonski, *American Troubadour* (New York: Henry Holt & Co., 1999), 85.
3. Frederick Lewis Allen, "There Is Radio Music in the Air," in *Only Yesterday: An Informal History of the 1920s* (New York: Harper & Row, 1931), 65.
4. Streissguth, *Say It with Music*, 44.

Chapter 8

1. Doris Eaton Travis with Joseph Eaton, Charles Eaton, and J. R. Morrs. *The Days We Danced: The Story of My Theatrical Family from Florenz Ziegfeld to Arthur Murray and Beyond* (Norman: University of Oklahoma Press, 2003), 65, 78.
2. Michael Freedland, *Irving Berlin* (New York: Stein and Day, 1974), 105.

Chapter 9

1. Philip Furia, *Irving Berlin: A Life in Song* (New York: Schirmer Books, 1998), 129.
2. Irving Berlin to Cole Porter, 1933, Cole Porter Collection, box 49, folder 302, Irving S. Gilmore Music Library, Yale University.
3. Irving Berlin to Cole Porter, telegram, January 4, 1949, Cole Porter Collection, box 49, folder 302, Irving S. Gilmore Music Library, Yale University.
4. New Yorker, n.d., 1925, referenced in Jablonski, *American Troubadour*, 113.
5. *New York Telegraph*, March 11, 1926.
6. Furia, *Irving Berlin*, 134.

Chapter 10

1. Jablonski, *American Troubadour,* 149.
2. Richard Corliss, "That Old Feeling: A Berlin bio-pic," *Time,* December 30, 2001, content.time.com/time/arts/article/0,8599,190220,00.html.
3. Furia, *Irving Berlin,* 157.
4. Clara Wilson-Hawken, "Ethel Waters Contemplates Her Own Vocal Style," The Black Sound and the Archive Working Group, campuspress.yale.edu/bsaw/bsaw-exhibition-start-here/ethel-waters-contemplates-her-own-vocal-style, offers background about the performer.
5. "Easter Parade by Fred Astaire," Songfacts, songfacts.com/facts/fred-astaire/easter-parade.
6. Rob Nixon, "Behind the Camera," TCM.com, May 3, 2006, https://www.tcm.com/articles/Programming%20Article/133542/behind-the-camera.
7. Daily Express, n.d., 1938, referenced in Jablonski, *American Troubadour,* 191.
8. Jablonski, *American Troubadour,* 146.

Chapter 11

1. "Behind the Songs," Irving Berlin, irvingberlin.com/behind-the-songs.
2. Furia, *Irving Berlin,* 193.
3. New York Times, July 11, 1940.
4. Sheryl Kaskowitz, *God Bless America: The Surprising History of an Iconic Song* (New York: Oxford University Press, 2013).
5. *Fort Wayne Sentinel,* October 24, 1940.
6. Chuck Miller, "The History and Legacy of 'God Bless America'," Chuck the Writer, July 3, 2010, https://chuckthewriter.blog/2010/07/03/the-history-and-legacy-of-god-bless-america/.

Chapter 12

1. *Saturday Evening Post,* January 14, 1944.

Chapter 13

1. *New York Times,* May 17, 1942.
2. Jablonski, *American Troubadour,* 208.
3. Ibid, 207.
4. Laurence Bergreen, *As Thousands Cheer: The Life of Irving Berlin* (New York: Penguin Books, 1990), 412.
5. Ibid, 441.

Chapter 14

1. William A. Everett and Paul R. Laird, *The Cambridge Companion to the Musical* (Cambridge: Cambridge University Press, 2002), 137.
2. Charlotte Greenspan, *Pick Yourself Up: Dorothy Fields and the American Musical* (New York: Oxford University Press, 2010).
3. Furia, *Irving Berlin*, 220.
4. Ibid., 231.
5. Papers of Kurt Weill and Lotte Lenya, box 48, folder 20, Irving S. Gilmore Music Library, Yale University.
6. Jablonski, *American Troubadour*, 247.

Chapter 15

1. Furia, *Irving Berlin*, 25.
2. *St. Louis Star-Times*, December 20, 1942.
3. *New York World Telegraph*, October 1, 1933.
4. "Elvis Presley," Wikipedia, wikipedia.org/wiki/Elvis_Presley.
5. Jablonski, *American Troubadour*, 254.
6. Ibid, 257.
7. Ibid, 297.
8. Harold Rome Papers, box 80, folder 2, Irving S. Gilmore Music Library, Yale University.
9. Jablonski, *American Troubadour*, 259.
10. Goddard Lieberson Papers, box 42, folder13, Irving S. Gilmore Music Library, Yale University.
11. E.Y. Harburg Collection, box 22, folder 174, Irving S. Gilmore Music Library, Yale University.
12. Laurence Bergreen, *As Thousands Cheer: The Life of Irving Berlin* (New York: Penguin Books, 1990).

Glossary

Annie Oakley She was a sharpshooter from rural Ohio. At age fifteen, she shocked audiences by winning a shooting match against traveling show marksman Frank Butler. The duo eventually toured the country as part of Buffalo Bill's Wild West Show. She was prominent in an almost all-male sport of sharpshooting. Irving Berlin based *Annie Get Your Gun* on her life.

Bowery In the early twentieth century, a street in New York City's East Village known for its saloons, burlesque theaters, vaudeville shows, criminal gangs, and nightlife. In later decades, the street was infamous for its large homeless population as well as punk rock bands. Today, the street is gentrified.

Burlesque A performance popular in the 1800s and early 1900s that combined satire, lewd comedy, and female stripteases. It was often presented in cabarets and music halls and theaters providing adult entertainment.

Camp Upton A training base and point of embarkation for the US army during World War I located in Yaphank, Long Island in Suffolk County, New York. Irving Berlin served here when he wrote *This Is the Army*, which was performed by the camp to raise money for the war effort. Sadly, during World War II, it was used to incarcerate Japanese-Americans.

Fanny Brice An American singer and comedienne headlining *Ziegfeld Follies* for many seasons. She performed Irving Berlin's "Sadie Salome (Go Home)" at Berlin's Music Box Theatre in a variety of productions. Her comical rendition, performed in a Yiddish accent, made the song a hit. Barbra Streisand portrayed her in the hit film *Funny Girl*.

Friars Club Founded in 1904 in New York City, the private club hosts musicians, comedians, and show business personalities among others. Irving Berlin and his mentor George Cohan were early members. Berlin wrote "Alexander's Ragtime Band" for the club's *Friars Frolics* in 1911.

George Cohan A composer, lyricist, actor, singer, and dancer best known for his patriotic songs "Over There," "Give My Regards to Broadway," "Yankee Doodle Boy," and "You're a Grand Old Flag." He was Berlin's mentor. His life is depicted in the film *Yankee Doodle Dandy*. His statue stands in the heart of Times Square.

Lower East Side In the early nineteenth century, it was known as Klein Deutschland or "Little Germany" due to the high number of German residents. By the late 1800s, it was the most densely packed neighborhood in the world. At that time, it included modern-day East Village, Chinatown, and Alphabet City.

Music Box A theater constructed in 1921 to house Irving Berlin and Sam Harris's *Music Box Revue*. Berlin produced many shows here, as did the Gershwin brothers and Cole Porter. Today, it still houses hit Broadway musicals like *Dear Evan Hansen*.

Newsie A newsboy selling newspapers and yelling headlines to passersby on the street to grab interest. Most worked long hours for little pay. A famous strike was featured in the musical *Newsies*.

Perle Mesta An American socialite who was known as the "Hostess with the Mostess" for her elegant Washington, DC parties. She inherited a fortune from her oil-rich father and through donations to Harry Truman's campaigns was appointed US ambassador to Luxembourg. Berlin's *Call Me Madam* is based on her story.

Pluggers Before radio, music publishers or stores relied on pluggers to sing or play on the piano new songs for the public in order to raise interest and to garner new songs. Pluggers would sings in cafés, restaurants, and street corners. The objective was to sell more sheet music to interested listeners.

Pogrom The term is most associated with Jews in Russia who were often killed or lost their homes and possessions in organized attacks.

Progressive Era The period of 1890-1920 marked by sweeping changes in labor laws, tenement housing improvements, women's suffrage, passage of personal income tax, land conservation, innovations like settlement houses where reformers would live among those whom they served, animal rights organizations like the Humane Society, infrastructure, and using data to advance a policy argument.

Ragtime A form of music popular from 1895 to 1919 emanating from Black musicians like Scott Joplin. Ragtime has a syncopated or ragged rhythm often with a catchy tune. Irving Berlin leveraged this new type of music for his smash hit "Alexander's Ragtime Band." He would be hailed as "the ragtime king," angering purists like Joplin who felt the public misunderstood what ragtime was.

Scott Joplin An American composer and pianist who is known for the "Maple Leaf Rag." His music heavily influenced Irving Berlin's early pieces. Joplin's music was revived in the 1970s with the hit film *The Sting*.

Tin Pan Alley A block in Manhattan's 28th Street between 5th and 6th Avenues where prominent music publishers, songwriters, singers, and producers congregated. It gained its title for the banging of pianos, which sounded like the banging of pans to passersby. Irving Berlin pitched his first hit songs to music publishers here. The area was known for its music production from 1885 to the 1930s.

Vaudeville A theatrical genre emanating from France and becoming popular in the US from the 1880s to the early 1930s. Performances often involved unrelated acts like singers, dancers, comedians, and physical acts like jugglers or athletes. It dominated the US entertainment scene for decades.

Vitaphone Founded in 1925, Warner Brothers' Vitaphone changed feature films forever. Prior, all films were silent and usually performed with live piano accompaniment. Early talkies like the *Jazz Singer* used the Vitaphone.

Woody Guthrie An American singer-songwriter from Oklahoma who was famous for counterculture songs and folk music like "This Land Is Your Land," *Dust Bowl Ballads*, and children's songs. He inspired singers like Bob Dylan, Bob Weir, and Johnny Cash among others. He objected to what he saw as Irving Berlin's overly patriotic or sentimental songs and commercialism. He stood in contrast with communist and folk-themed songs.

References

Books

Bergreen, Laurence. *As Thousands Cheer: The Life of Irving Berlin.* New York: Penguin Books, 1990.

Furia, Philip. *Irving Berlin: A Life in Song.* New York: Schirmer Books, 1998.

Jablonski, Edward. *American Troubadour.* New York: Henry Holt & Co., 1999.

Kimmelman, Leslie, and David Gardner. *Write On, Irving Berlin!* Ann Arbor, MI: Sleeping Bear Press, 2018.

Sears, Benjamin (voice), and Bradford Connor (piano). Liner notes. *Keep on Smiling: Songs by Irving Berlin, 1915-198.* Oakton Recordings, 1996. CD.

Streissguth, Tom. *Say It with Music: A Story about Irving Berlin.* Minneapolis: Carolrhoda Books, Inc., 1994.

Travis, Doris, and J. R. Morris. *The Days We Danced: The Story of My Theatrical Family from Florenz Ziegfeld to Arthur Murray and Beyond.* Norman, OK: University of Oklahoma Press, 2003.

Wilk, Max. *They're Playing Our Song: Conversations with America's Classic Songwriters.* New York: Atheneum, 1973.

Documentaries

Irving Berlin: The Voice of the City. BBC Bristol and A&E Network, 1988.

Archival and Manuscript Collections

Cole Porter Collection, Irving S. Gilmore Music Library, Yale University.

E.Y. Harburg Collection, Irving S. Gilmore Music Library, Yale University.

Prints and Photographs Division. Library of Congress.

Periodicals

Catton, Bruce. "He Wanted to Murder the Bugler." *American Heritage* 18, no. 5 (August 1967).

Plays

Call Me Madam. Revival of original 1950 Broadway production. Music and lyrics by Irving Berlin. New York City Center. New York, NY, February 2019.

Hershey Felder as Irving Berlin. Created by Hershey Felder. 59E59 Theaters. New York, NY, 2018.

Websites

American Classics, found online at Americanclassicsmusic.org.

Turner Classic movies, found online at TCM.com.

Lectures

Dan Egan, Lecturer at Yale University of the American Musical, Yale Club, February 2019.

Index